AWAKENING
The Sleeping
GIANT
The Church and the Road to Revival

Mario C. Alleckna

Requests for information should be addressed to:
    Trafford Publishing, Suite 6E - 2333 Government St.
    Victoria BC V8T 4P4

All Scripture quotations from King James Version

Typography: Brian Rodda Visuals
Cover design: Mario C. Alleckna
Cover finish: Jonas Plouffe
Cover photo: © Copyright Bernard Hulshof, www.weatherpictures.nl ; used with permission

National Library of Canada Cataloguing in Publication Data

Alleckna, Mario C., 1956-
    Awakening the sleeping giant : the church and the road to revival / Mario C. Alleckna.
ISBN 1-4120-0171-4
1. Christian life. I. Title.
BV4501.3.A44 2003   248.4   C2003-902035-5

TRAFFORD

This book was published *on-demand* **in cooperation with Trafford Publishing.**
On-demand publishing is a unique process and service of making a book available for retail sale to the public taking advantage of on-demand manufacturing and Internet marketing. **On-demand publishing** includes promotions, retail sales, manufacturing, order fulfilment, accounting and collecting royalties on behalf of the author.

Suite 6E, 2333 Government St., Victoria, B.C. V8T 4P4, CANADA
Phone   250-383-6864   Toll-free   1-888-232-4444 (Canada & US)
Fax   250-383-6804   E-mail   sales@trafford.com
Web site   www.trafford.com   TRAFFORD PUBLISHING IS A DIVISION OF TRAFFORD HOLDINGS LTD.
Trafford Catalogue #03-0539   www.trafford.com/robots/03-0539.html

10   9

*To my Saviour Jesus
with deepest gratitude
for His forever love and
forgiveness.*

CONTENTS

Acknowledgements

First of all, thank You my wonderful Saviour for giving me life, hope and strength, and for being my inspiration. I have nothing without You Jesus!

Thank You Lord for using people to help us, encourage and motivate us. This book would not have been possible without the love, prayers and support of my home group. Garry and Patti Wells you are not only great leaders and true lovers of Jesus; thank you for also being my greatest cheer leaders.

And then there are those who helped put it all together. Thank you Erica Robinson and Kristi Carruthers for being such great editors, and for your incredible patience with me. I could never have done this work without you! Ron Gray, your contribution as editor was a special blessing!

Last but not least, my wonderful family. Thanks to my precious wife Pauline for hanging in there with me, and for giving me some valuable hints and insights; to Benny for encouraging and helping me, and for being the son and friend that you are; to all of my wonderful children for making me the blessed Dad that I am.

I love you all!

Mario Alleckna
Chilliwack, B.C.

Introduction
Drug Busts in the Bible Belt

IT WAS ON A FRIDAY, when the local Chilliwack newspaper once again announced the police raid on a few marijuana grow operations. This kind of police work had been going on for many years, appearing in the news on a weekly basis. It used to be that these "grow-ops" were located at some secluded place somewhere up in the surrounding mountains, or at a farm outside of town, but things have changed. The cultivation of marijuana plants has become a growing business venture in every part of our city. Last year police seized a $40 million ecstasy outfit from a sophisticated laboratory in the basement of a nice family home. This drug in tablet form is very popular among young people, and used mainly by ravers and other all night dance partiers. With a drug problem comes, naturally, a host of other crimes. Those who are addicted, in order to satisfy their habit, have to come up with quite a bit of money. These people are usually not capable of holding a steady nine to five job. Prostitution, armed robberies, break-ins, purse snatchings and car thefts, become therefore a regular part of our daily news. More violent crimes, such as beatings, knife attacks, and even homicides, can be added to the list. Are you wondering what all of this might have to do with the church and revival? First of all, let me say that the above is not a description of your typical big city environment. This comes straight from the "Bible belt".

Living east of Vancouver, Canada, in a community of about 65,000 people, we are blessed with more than 68 churches, including a variety of different denominations. The number of congregations indicates that there must be thousands of Christians in Chilliwack. What a concentration of the Holy Spirit! Just imagine the amount of prayer going up to Heaven in one week. But, how can it be that, with such an army of God's people present, there seems to be no difference between this part of the world and other crime stricken cities? Where is the life-changing power of God manifested through the church? What is wrong, what is missing? Has Christianity, through the compromise of values and by adjusting to world standards, become just another philosophy? Could it be that we, as Christians, are too busy trying to fix our own problems, such as marriage break-ups, church splits, financial struggles, and burnout; when we should be utilizing the power of the Holy Spirit, setting our cities on fire for Jesus? Can we turn a whole nation over to Christ? One thing we do know, God is able to change the world in which we live, and He has chosen to do His work through us, the church.

In the following chapters of this book, I will attempt to give some clues for the dilemma of the Christian church, who finds herself without the power to change the world around her.

Part I
A Church Without Power

Chapter 1

The Professional, Modern Church and the Deception

IN THE YEAR OF 1996, a group of young people from New Zealand came to visit our church. Getting to know them, I found out that they felt called by the Lord to be missionaries in this part of our country. Now wait a minute, missionaries in the "Bible belt"? Yeah, right! Everybody knows that missionaries go to Africa and Papua New Guinea or Brazil. After all, this is the professional church. We have Christian schools, Bible colleges, spiritual seminars and conferences, lectures, special courses, and home Bible studies. Don't forget our Christian bookstores and libraries with books, magazines, videos and all kinds of study material.

Yet, these people from New Zealand were sincere in their walk with God. Their decision to come as missionaries to Canada wasn't just a spontaneous idea without any prayer behind it. Were they maybe overzealous or not hearing quite right when God spoke? And what if God really sent them to open our eyes to some hard facts? Has the highly educated, modern church been blinded? Could it be that these accomplishments of our modern-day church are filled with great deception? Is it possible that, without realizing it, we have added a little bit of Jesus to our many programs rather than adding a little bit of program to our Jesus?

Never before in history has the church been

more educated than today in the computer Bible age. Where it used to be sufficient to have a basic knowledge and understanding of God's Word, we are now faced with a mountain of books, commentaries, study guides and videos on many Bible topics. What a difference when we look at the early church! But let's be honest, has all of this knowledge changed our hearts or mainly filled our heads? Someone once said, the bigger our heads the less we are able to dream; which reminds me of the Scripture in *Matthew 18:3, where Jesus tells His disciples that no one will enter heaven unless he or she becomes like a child. Could this mean that the level of our maturity as Christians correlates directly with our childlikeness toward our heavenly Father? The following is the apostle Paul's view on the subject:

*Matt. 18:3: Verily I say unto you, except ye are converted, and become as little children, ye shall not enter into the kingdom of heaven.

> "And if any man think that he knoweth anything, he knoweth nothing yet as he ought to know. Knowledge puffeth up, but love edifieth" (1Cor.8:2,1).

Education sharpens our minds but it often dulls our hearts. Too much head knowledge can lead to an intellectualization of our relationship with God, which eventually could close the door of our hearts. I believe that, just like overeating doesn't make a fast runner, (remember, we're supposed to run a race... **Hebrews 12:1), so Christian over-education has, in many ways, paralysed the church. On a nutritional level, too many vitamins can be harmful.

**Heb. 12:1: ... and let us run with patience the race that is set before us.

When we look at the people who hated and

opposed Jesus and His supporters the most, we see that they were the scholars who knew all the Scriptures in and out. They even wore them around their necks.

At the other end of the scale, there is Peter, a simple fisherman with a calling from God. About three thousand people accepted Christ as their Saviour, after he preached a very basic sermon (*Acts 2:41).

It wasn't Peters' eloquent speech or a possible degree in theology that determined his success; it was rather the King's invisible signet ring of divine authority Peter was wearing, and the supernatural, spiritual energy that flowed from the words he spoke. The apostle Paul said it this way:

*Acts 2:41: Then they that gladly received his word were baptized, and the same day there were added unto them about three thousand souls.

"And I, brethren, when I came to you, came not with excellency of speech or of wisdom, declaring unto you the testimony of God. For I determined not to know anything among you, save Jesus Christ, and Him crucified. And my speech and my preaching was not with enticing words of man's wisdom, but in demonstration of the Spirit and of power: That your faith should not stand in the wisdom of men, but in the power of God" (1Cor.2:1,2,4,5).

The message of the cross in its powerful simplicity, when presented in the divine anointing of God's Holy Spirit, is the transforming truth that changes lives forever. One of the greatest deceptions in our modern church is overintellectualizing; the more knowledge we have, the better we think we can serve God. I am sure this is going to cause a few eyebrows to raise when in the last days more and more children will prophesy (**Joel 2:28).

**Joel 2:28: And it shall come to pass afterward, that I will pour out my Spirit upon all flesh; and your sons and your daughters shall prophesy.

After all, our relationship with Jesus Christ is a heart issue, not a head issue!

A big dilemma that comes with pride in education is complacency. We feel that we are doing just fine as Christians because we are working so hard to become educated. It seems, the more we think we know about Him, the less we see the need to seek Him. In other words, we stop pressing onward and are hindered from being open to radical changes, questioning our walk and our position.

But all this "busy-ness", with seminars, special courses, programs and meetings, goes in the wrong direction. It appears that we have institutionalized the church, and instead of just pursuing God, we began to pursue the well-intended idea of establishing the perfect church. And, while we are trying so hard to run the professional church, we easily become too busy to run after Christ. Our once strong vision and calling to be a radical follower of Jesus, devoted to a life of prayer and intercession, and driven by an unquenchable thirst for His presence, often end up getting lost in a mountain of daily tasks. Through the invention and implementation of all kinds of strategies, and motivated by our eagerness to build a well-functioning church, we have in many cases become servants of programs. We go all-out trying to find ways to make church fun, exciting and relevant, while becoming more and more consumed by the demands of modern-day church business. Now, realizing that church business has a lot to do with people, they might end up becoming our main focus. Seeking to accommodate everybody, we so easily become people-pleasers.

"For do I now persuade men, or God? Or do I seek to please men? For if I yet pleased men, I should not be the servant of Christ" (Gal.1:10).

It is little wonder that some churches are rapidly growing. Their programs and the ways they cater to people seem irresistible. Unfortunately, instead of leading new converts into God's presence, where all their real needs would be met, we point them to the "right" program.

We have placed such an emphasis on accommodating people, that we don't realize how the Holy Spirit is kept outside the door. After all, is there a real need for His Presence when we have small-groups, meetings and fellowship-events with great programs and all the answers? In fact, would we even want His Presence? Perhaps He might change the way we do church?

Today the office of a Pastor is pursued much like any other career–with some formal training and a degree at the end. This training commonly involves subjects such as speech-making and how to do a professional presentation. (Let's remember what Paul had to say about "eloquent speaking"; 1Cor.2:1) Simple fishermen with a calling from God would not easily qualify for a position in today's highly educated church. And while believers are hearing the Word of God, presented in a professional way (a funny story here and there is sure to enhance the experience), they starve while sitting at His banquet table. This explains why in recent years thousands of seasoned and mature believers have left the organized church. A. W. Tozer's words still ring true: "There is today no lack of Bible teachers to set forth correctly the principles of the doctrines of Christ, but too many of these seem satisfied to teach the fundamentals of the faith year after year, strangely unaware that there is in their ministry no manifest Presence, nor anything unusual in their personal lives." Who are today's church-leaders? How do they live? Are they the kind of peculiar people the Bible talks about and do they carry a strong, spiritual anointing?

Contrary to Jesus and the powerful Bible Teachers and Revivalists of the past, who all preached repentance, most church-leaders today think that showing God's love means we are here to make people feel good. The overemphasis that is placed on God's grace has caused a terrible imbalance in today's teachings. Vital issues such as repentance and the fear of the Lord are not easily addressed in an environment created for comfort.

"Think not that I am come to send peace on earth: I came not to send peace, but a sword" (Matt.10:34).

Like it or not, the almighty, righteous and sovereign God of the whole universe does not fit into a box with "grace only" written on it!

The extreme focus on people that we see in today's church is also found in the philosophy of Humanism, where man becomes the centre, and God is there to fulfil man's desires. This has resulted in the creation of the absolutely unbiblical "prosperity Gospel" with the 'bless me'–'bless me' attitude. Instead of desiring God's presence we constantly ask for His presents. Quite a few books have been written on how the Lord will prosper you if you pray a certain prayer over and over. Soon our focus becomes "easy living" rather than "right living". But the fact is, we were created to be *with* Him, and not just to receive *from* Him. God's desire is to spend quality time with His children.

Still, many church-leaders seem to think that, preaching a challenging and convicting message was for the John The Baptist's, and the Wesley's and Finney's of the past. Could it also be that the worldly desires and ambitions of believers are never questioned by our church-leaders because they themselves have become entangled with worldly comforts?

Nevertheless, operating the church like a business with administration, accounting, building programs, counsellor services and our own web sites, makes us also very vulnerable to focusing on money. The budget of some bigger facilities goes into the hundreds of thousands of dollars, which could translate into some major financial pressures. And since the main source for church income again is people, the number of attendants is of great importance and still seems to be the measure of church success. Quantity instead of quality is generally the focus. And, with the incredible task of building and running a professional church comes the aspect of "taking control", which adds a whole new dimension to our problem.

The implementation of strategies and programs may give us a sense of accomplishment and success, but really, the only thing that will bring empowerment and victory to God's people is the transforming presence of His manifest Glory in the church.

Our relationship with Jesus Christ is a heart issue, not a head issue.

Chapter 2

The Drive to Control

WHAT IS IT THAT MOTIVATES US to do the things we do and the way we do them? What drives us to take control of our lives, our businesses, our ministries etc.? There are two main areas at which I would like to look. The first one has to do with the society we live in, a society of success-driven "doers". The other is a deep-rooted psychological issue, "the ancient fear".

One of the slogans, in the light of economic success, in our North American culture, is to "just do it!" We feel that, "standing still means going backward", and that we need to increase the productivity, develop new markets, be innovative, plan ahead, beat the competition, and do, do, do...

When the first settlers came from Europe, they came with great determination to succeed. They worked very hard, pursuing their goals and dreams. Today this mentality is still one of our culture's main building blocks. Take your life into your hands, work hard and be successful! In those days, for many people, it was pure survival. Today it seems more like the picture of a mouse on a treadmill or as the Bible puts it, "the more they have the more they want" (*Ecc. 5:10).

However, the "doer" mentality seems to be in our genes, to the point where many suffer from burnout or being workaholics. Even our free time is planned to the minute. More and more psychosomatic illnesses, and the ever-increasing demand for stress management programs, speak for themselves.

*Ecc. 5:10: He that loveth silver shall not be satisfied with silver; nor he that loveth abundance with increase...

*Ps.27:14; 46:10:
Wait on the Lord.
Be still, and know
that I am God.

No wonder we don't do too well when it comes to some of the Bible's most profound requests such as, "wait on the Lord" or "be still" (*Ps.27:14; 46:10). Waiting patiently on the Lord with quiet contentment, allowing God's plans to unfold in His timing, seems to be one of our greatest challenges.

While in someone's office, I came across a little "blurb" hanging on the wall. It went something like this: "Please don't ask me to relax, it is my 'busy-ness' that holds me together." Here, we find yet another aspect of why keeping busy has become one of the major drugs of our Western society. Doing also distracts us from a deep psychological problem.

I believe that much of what we see as human behaviour is based on a mostly hidden insecurity, which finds its roots in an even deeper sense of fear; (the fear of failure, of loneliness and abandonment, the fear of being rejected, the fear of the unknown, the unpredictable–and the list goes on). There is a longing in all of us to feel safe, to feel good about ourselves, to be accepted and to belong. Maybe that is why loneliness is such a hard emotion to deal with. Since this kind of fear lies hidden within us and seems to be no respecter of persons, regardless of their cultural background, gender, or religion; I came to the conclusion, that it must have its origin way back at the beginning of mankind. In other words, Adam and Eve passed it on. That is why I call it "the ancient fear".

Now, let us try to put ourselves into Adam and Eve's shoes for a minute...Life in the garden was perfect. They didn't have to work to make a living, and they didn't have to be afraid of anything. In fact, they didn't even know what fear meant until they ate the forbidden fruit (*Gen. 3:6,7). All of their security was taken away when they were kicked out of the garden because sin had entered the human race (**Gen.3:24). And since they had eaten from the tree, their eyes were open to the hard facts of life outside of the safety they had enjoyed. The realization of their nakedness, their helplessness, guilt and shame, must have produced a deep sense of insecurity, even fear in Adam and Eve. "How are we going to live now, what are we going to do...?" Not to forget the awful feeling of having done something that really upset the Father. After all, Adam and Eve were real people. Looking at our own lives, our worries and our insecurities, we find that they are not much different. ("How am I going to pay that bill, what am I going to do...?") When we read the Scriptures it appears that Adam and Eve didn't have much time to get emotionally and physically prepared for the event either, which only added to the pressure. When Dad kicked them out, they where basically thrown into the cold water.

We can easily see that it isn't just our sinfulness we inherited from Adam and Eve but also the insecurity that it produces. And just as sin seems to cling to us like a dirty shirt–Paul put it this way: "I hate what I do, and I do what I hate", Rom. 7:15–so also our insecurities cling to us.

The bottom line is, it is our helplessness, our separation from the Father and His safety-giving presence, that causes us to be fearful. And it is our guilt and shame that cause us to be insecure. Sooner or later we will all have to deal with fear and insecurities in our lives. We were not

*Gen.3:6,7:And when the woman saw that the tree was good for food, and that it was pleasant to the eyes, and a tree to be desired to make one wise, she took of the fruit thereof, and did eat, and gave also unto her husband with her; and he did eat. And the eyes of them both were opened, and they knew that they were naked.

**Gen. 3:24: So He drove out the man.

created to be separated from our Creator and there will never be complete peace as long as we are. Fear is not, and never was, part of God's plan for mankind (*Is.41:10;**Ps.27:1,3), but the fact that the Lord puts so much emphasis on this subject in His Word, shows that it is real and relevant.

*Is. 41:10: Fear thou not; for I am with thee.

**Ps. 27:1,3: The Lord is my light and my salvation; whom shall I fear? Though an host should camp against me, my heart shall not fear.

But our longing to feel safe and to feel good about ourselves, to be accepted, and even loved, makes us very vulnerable to get onto the wrong path as we subconsciously try to avoid having to face our weakness, our "nakedness", guilt and shame.

How then do most people keep on top of their fear? They distract themselves with a busy and active lifestyle, by complying with certain society standards in order to be accepted, and by developing a sense of strength and independence. In other words, by "taking control". This gives a feeling of security and in the end even a sense of accomplishment and power. (Often the follower type person depends on the security and power of control–someone else's that is–as can be seen in many co-dependent relationships.)

I need to remind us of our adversary, satan, who will always try to use any kind of weakness in a person's life, to draw that person away from God. Fear and insecurity are a great field for his schemes. In his very subtle way satan either tries to drive people into a state of anxiety, hopelessness and depression, or he convinces them that there is no need to be afraid. "No fear" is an idea that even the fashion industry promotes. Just take control, you don't need anybody, you can be strong and self-sufficient. It is one of societies' greatest deceptions when people become oblivious to their need for a Creator God, replacing Him with their own independence. If people would openly face their helplessness and their insecurities, they might begin to search for help. This could lead them to God, which is not exactly what satan has in mind (*Prov.1:33).

*Prov. 1:33: But whoso hearkeneth unto me shall dwell safely, and shall be quiet from fear of evil.

When we look at our society today we see the negative impact of the "don't have fear" attitude. No fear of the Lord, no fear of any consequences resulting from one's own actions, nor even a fear to die.

Christian or non-Christian, because of our "doer" mentality we so easily fall into the trap of "taking control". It is when we don't have any influence on our circumstances, when things are out of our control, that fear and insecurity begin to surface. Trying to get into a position of control is usually the first thing we do in dealing with a situation. How many times, before we even think of praying, as we struggle with a challenge, have we taken a problem into our own hands?!

The impact of "taking control" affects all areas of our lives. Taking control for instance, produces impatience. I believe, that is where a slogan like "help yourself and then God will help you" comes from. Once we've developed the "doer" mentality and have taken control of our lives, it becomes hard to patiently wait on the Lord. We get anxious to accomplish our goals.

But the biggest problem with all of this is: the more we take control as Christians, instead of completely surrendering to God at all times and in every circumstance, the more our focus on Jesus decreases. As we take charge, we begin to live in our own strength, and by our own understanding, instead of trusting the Lord, and living by faith (*Heb.10:38). We might even develop an attitude of legalism, which causes us to become more and more religious.

Put together in a formula, our problem would look like this: Taking control can lead to legalism, which produces self-righteousness; creating a deceptive feeling of security, causing us to say, "I don't need to change or question myself, I'm doing quite all right." And since we have a real enemy called satan, who roams around like a lion seeking to devour us, we can be sure that these philosophies will aid him in his work (**1 Pet. 5:8).

*Heb.10:38: Now the just shall live by faith.

**1 Pet.5:8: Be sober, be vigilant; because your adversary the devil, as a roaring lion, walketh about, seeking-whom he may devour.

**Waiting patiently
on the Lord with quiet contentment, allowing God's plans to
unfold in His timing, seems to
be one of our greatest
challenges.**

Chapter 3

Legalism - Self-Righteousness - Pride

PRIME EXAMPLES of the L.S.P. dilemma were the Pharisees. They were the religious leaders in Jesus' days, which put them in a strong position of control. As the Masters of legalism, they added more than six hundred home-made rules and regulations to the Torah, God's law given through Moses. By adding and trying to follow all of these rules, they pushed themselves into a feeling of holiness–which, of course, was nothing but self-righteousness. To think how much effort it must have taken to live a life full of rituals, and to work so hard trying to achieve holiness, it is easy to imagine that these legalists took great pride in their accomplishments. And did the Pharisees ever feel great until Jesus came and shook up their legalistic, self-righteous world!

One of many examples in the Bible, concerning a legalistic attitude, is recorded in the book of *Luke, in chapter 19 verses 39 and 40. When Jesus came riding into Jerusalem, some of the Pharisees told Him to rebuke His disciples because they were making so much noise praising God. They must have had a very strict noise bylaw back then! Jesus replied that the stones would cry out if they didn't.

Another story that illustrates that legalism, self-righteousness and pride are "close friends" is found in **Luke, 13:10 to 16. Here we can see how the chemistry of pride works as a heart hardener. The leader of the synagogue in which Jesus was teaching rebuked Him for healing a

*Lk.19:39,40: And some of the Pharisees from among the multitude said unto Him, Master, rebuke Thy disciples. And He answered and said unto them, I tell you that, if these should hold their peace, the stones would immediately cry out.

**Lk.13:13,14: And He laid His hands on her: and immediately she was made straight, and glorified God. And the ruler of the synagogue answered with indignation, because that Jesus had healed on the Sabbath day.

woman on a Sabbath. The priest obviously cared more about "the rules" than about that poor woman.

The religious authorities during Jesus' time here on earth, are extreme examples of what "taking control" can lead to in the end. They thought themselves closer to God than anyone else; and yet their legalistic, self-righteous and prideful ways caused their hearts to grow hard and cold. Blinded by their own idea of what truth is, they were walking in darkness, unable to see that the living truth was standing right in front of them.

It is critical for us today, to recognize our own weakness and the deception that hides behind every corner (*Lk. 21:8; **Rev.20:10). Many leaders of countries once founded on Biblical principles, instead of continually relying on God, have chosen to make their armed forces as well as a strong economy the main foundation for the welfare and security of their nation.

When we take control as Christians, we may just lose sight of what the Lord wants to do. This also could result in a vicious cycle. The more we develop a sense of responsibility for the success of our ministries; the more we put ourselves under a self-inflicted pressure "to make things work". The financial obligations of a ministry easily feed into this problem, as we saw earlier. It doesn't take much for us to forget who the Author, not only of our faith, but also of our ministries, is.

The "doer" mentality makes it very hard to "let go and let God"..., and an over-eagerness to do God's work can easily distract us from the essentially important intimacy with Him.

*Lk.21:8: And He said, Take heed that ye be not deceived.

**Rev.20:10: And the devil that deceived them was cast into the lake of fire.

Most of us are familiar with the story of Mary and Martha from the book of *Luke chapter 10. Here we find that eager performance often hinders us from sitting at Jesus' feet.

With all good intentions and great excitement, we develop programs and strategies, spending hundreds of hours in meetings in order to become most efficient. And when things don't seem to work as smoothly as we expected, we decide that another professional seminar and some books and videos on the subject are needed.

We have given into our North-American "doer" mentality, because sitting and carefully listening doesn't seem very appealing to a man who takes great pride in his own accomplishments. And while an active church-life gives us a gratifying sense of achievement, we are too busy to sit at His feet.

Meanwhile, in a not so highly educated and professional part of our world, the whole congregation of a church comes under the healing anointing of the Holy Spirit after a little boy walks up to the pulpit saying, "Jesus is here". All those who were sick in that congregation were miraculously healed on that day.

*Lk.10:38-42: Now it came to pass, as they went, that He entered into a certain village: and a certain woman named Martha received Him into her house. And she had a sister called Mary, which also sat at Jesus' feet, and heard His Word. But Martha was cumbered about much serving, and came to Him, and said, Lord, dost Thou not care that my sister hath left me to serve alone? Bid her therefore that she help me. And Jesus answered and said unto her, Martha, Martha, thou art careful and troubled about many things: But one thing is needful: and Mary hath chosen that good part, which shall not be taken away from her.

Eager performance often hinders us from sitting at Jesus' feet.

Chapter 4

The Splits Syndrome

IN THIS CHAPTER, I need to address a subject which I believe to be the main reason for spiritual apathy in the church today "the splits syndrome". This is, when Christians try to stretch across the great divide between heaven and earth, in order to get the most out of both worlds. Before we get going, let us remember two very important facts. First of all, we are weak and vulnerable because of our sinful nature, and secondly, we have an invisible enemy: satan, who is very real, and who is trying to use any kind of weakness in our lives to deceive us, and to pull us away from the only source of life and truth, Jesus Christ.

Have you ever struggled as a Christian with some "worldly" desires? For some of us, there is the dream of a five star hotel holiday, a fancy sports car, or a big house with swimming pool and hot tub. Others wouldn't mind a nice yacht or some top of the line hunting gear, or maybe jewellery or a new, fashionable, wardrobe. I think we've all had our fair share of worldly desires in some way or another. Our desires may differ, since we are different from each other, but that's about all.

Having desires in itself is not wrong, but what if they are "worldly"?...; and what does that mean anyway? The answer to this question is quite simple when we look at the following two equations: Worldly equals Temporal and Mortal; Heavenly equals Eternal and Immortal.

There are two very different worlds in existence, and although they are as far apart as the east is from the west, there is no form of "no man's land" between them. It's either black or white! And with the two worlds come two views regarding life. God's view and this world's view. The next question is: where do our desires originate? Are they inspired by God, His Holy Spirit, or by our flesh nature, our worldliness?

When it comes to materialistic desires I guess it is safe to say that having "things" isn't necessarily bad, but what it takes to get them, usually is! The fact that it uses so much of our resources, such as time and money, to develop our lifestyles and then maintain them; shows how we are tied down and so very occupied with just that. And then there often is very little left for the work of God. We end up adding a little bit of Jesus to our lifestyles.

Coming back to our original question, what motivates us to store up treasures here on earth, when Jesus clearly told us to store up treasures in heaven where nothing can destroy them (*Matt.6:19-21)? Now, most of us would reply that we are also storing up in heaven by giving of our time and money to the various ministries; and here exactly lies our problem! By investing into the two very different Kingdoms, we are trying to get the most out of both worlds, which means, we are doing "the splits". Attempting to run "the race" (**Heb.12:1) with one foot in the world and the other foot in the Bible, we are serving two masters (***Matt.6:24), whether we like it or not. It is inevitable that our hearts become divided, and in the process of decision-making, our worldly comfort so often wins over investing more into God's Kingdom.

*Matt.6:19-21: Lay not up for yourselves treasures upon earth, where moth and rust doth corrupt, and where thieves break through and steal: But lay up for yourselves treasures in heaven, where neither moth nor rust doth corrupt, and where thieves do not break through nor steal: For where your treasure is, there will your heart be also.

**Heb.12:1: ... and let us run with patience the race that is set before us.

***Matt.6:24: No man can serve two masters: Ye cannot serve God and mammon.

Another good illustration of our problem is to see a deep canyon between God and this world. Those of us who want to enjoy the things that the world has to offer, and at the same time attempt to develop a meaningful relationship with Jesus Christ, have one foot on either side of the canyon. Looks pretty awkward and scary doesn't it? Try running a race that way!

But the "splits syndrome" isn't just a materialistic issue. It's also about trying to find happiness and fulfillment in this world, while at the same time asking God for His joy, love and peace. It gets really interesting, when we consider the two different world standards: We learn that "happy are the successful, the beautiful and the wealthy". In God's Word we learn that "happy are the righteous and holy".

The seriousness of our problem becomes even more evident when we look at certain Scriptures. When Jesus, as recorded by John in *Revelation 3:16, addresses the Church of Laodicea, He makes very clear how He feels about their lukewarm attitude, criticizing them for being "neither hot nor cold". Their half-heartedness made Him feel sick.

Do we really understand what it means to love the Lord our God with all of our heart, soul and might (**Deut.6:5)? Are we striving to seek His Kingdom first in everything we do (***Matt.6:33)? And what about our honesty with God? When we sing lines like, "I surrender all"...; or "I'm desperate for You"..., do we really mean that?

Let's face it! We can not possibly be sold out for Jesus, giving a hundred percent of our lives to Him, when at the same time we are trying so hard to be successful, beautiful and wealthy.

*Rev.3:16: So then because thou art lukewarm, and neither cold nor hot, I will spue thee out of my mouth.

**Deut.6:5: And thou shalt love the Lord thy God with all thine heart, and with all thy soul, and with all thy might.

***Matt.6:33: But seek ye first the kingdom of God and His righteousness.

When Jesus came to this earth, He gave all that He could give – His life. He deserves our very best of everything. This is what the world needs to see. May our conviction become our motivation!

I would like to end this chapter by quoting Dr. G. Campbell-Morgan who wrote these very challenging words:

> "If the church of God in the cities of today were aloof from the maxims of the age, separated from the materialistic philosophies of the schools, bearing her witness alone to the all sufficiency of Christ and the perfection of His salvation, even though persecuted and ostracized and bruised, it would be to the church that men would look in the hour of their heart break and sorrow and national need. The reason why men do not look to the church today, is that she has destroyed her own influence by compromise."

**Our worldly comfort
so often wins over investing
more into God's Kingdom.**

Chapter 5

Life Without the Right Focus is B. A. D.

LET ME BEGIN WITH A STATEMENT: That which we focus on in life, gets bigger and bigger and becomes our main purpose, and our motivation. At a young age we learn that "to be focused and to stay focused" is a very important thing. Our parents told us to concentrate on what we were doing in order to get things done, and done properly. Our teachers told us to stay focused during school assignments. If we are not focused we become distracted, losing sight of that which we want to accomplish.

As we try to walk our Christian walk we realize, that there are many distractions today making it hard to stay focused on our goal, which is to build a meaningful relationship with Jesus Christ. I would like to look at three areas that "cloud our vision".

First, it is our "**B**usy-ness", the hustle and bustle of trying to make a living, to provide for our families and to get ahead, that causes us to be stressed and tired out. Life has become so complex, that it seems almost impossible to escape the rat-race. Being overworked, we so easily end up in a state of **A**pathy. If we are not involved in constructive activities, we tend to spend our evenings in front of the "Square Entertainer"; too tired to enjoy some quality family time, or read the Bible, let alone to get engaged in some Christian outreach. In order to re-evaluate or even change the course of our lives, we would need mental and physical energy, which we don't have any more.

And then there is the power of **Deception**, making us feel that we are okay the way things are. We think we don't need to change or question our lifestyle. And if we are challenged to reflect on the *way* we live, we quickly calm ourselves by saying that we are not the only ones who live like that. We are just being normal. If you want to provide a good education for yourself or your kids, have a little extra and make sure your retirement is looked after, you've got to work hard and put in extra hours. That's just the *way* life is now.

What is wrong with that picture? There is basically no difference between the Christian or non-Christian lifestyle other than the Sunday morning church routine and the once a week Bible study. I believe that satan has managed to pull many Christians into a *way* of life that is dominated by the same standards that most people in our culture live by. We somehow have been deceived to think that we cannot or should not be radically different, which leads to a wrong focus in life. And since we live like the rest of the world, we consequently face the same problems that everybody else faces, such as divorce, financial struggles, family problems etc. "Defeated" and "paralysed" are terms that come to mind when we look at this sad picture.

But what can we do, and how could things change? The answer is, we need to make a decision to re-focus our lives! Let us look at the Bible, the "manual for living", for some instructions. When it comes to the question whether or not we should be radically different from the world; the easiest thing to do is to look at how Jesus and the disciples, or the believers of the early church, used to live. There is no Scripture indicating that we shouldn't take their way of living as an example.

So then, how did Jesus live; what occupied Him, what was His main focus in life? Maybe it is a little easier for us to relate to the disciples and the early church members, since they were ordinary people like us.

In the book of *Acts chapter 2 verses 44 and 45 we find a powerful example regarding the believers of the first church and their standard of living. Here it talks about their unity and how they looked after each other's needs. They sold their unnecessary possessions, gave to those who didn't have, and shared everything. What an example of Christ's love and compassion! I think they knew that to be self-sufficient is one of our greatest enemies; it is easy to see that independence leads to pride. Their focus was obviously to love the Lord and their neighbour above their earthly possessions. Radically different, I'd say! The result was that they grew greatly in numbers. Who wouldn't want to be part of that church?!

In our western culture we find that the main emphasis is on the desires and the outward things of the flesh, (just look at the magazines at the check-out in your grocery store). It's all about how you look, what kind of a car you drive, how much money you make, and who you know. Inner qualities, such as the respect and the integrity of a person, have become long-lost virtues in a society, sold out to the things of the flesh. As Christians we are called to be different from those who are driven by their fleshly nature:

*Acts 2:44,45: And all that believed were together, and had all things in common; And sold their possessions and goods, and parted them to all men, as every man had need.

"This I say then, walk in the Spirit, and ye shall not fulfil the lust of the flesh"(Gal.5:16).

Outward things mean nothing in God's economy, and in His Word the Lord makes very clear what we should strive for, and what our focus should be:

"Finally, brethren, whatsoever things are true, whatsoever things are honest, whatsoever things are just, whatsoever things are pure, whatsoever things are lovely, whatsoever things are of good report; if there be any virtue, and if there be any praise, think on these things"(Phil.4:8).

The Scripture in Romans 12:2 shows us an important step we must take in order to be able to live according to His will and to find freedom from the chains of the flesh:

"And be not conformed to this world; but be ye transformed by the renewing of your mind, that ye may prove what is that good, and acceptable, and perfect, will of God."

This definitely talks about a conscious decision on our part. We need to renew our minds. We must think differently, looking at life and this world in general, which will change our perspective and our focus.

But to be focused also means to see things clearly and undistorted. It all begins with a sincere and honest evaluation of our lives as Christians. What are our priorities, what has been our main focus, honestly? A good way to measure this is by looking at how much time, energy and money we've invested into different areas of our lives. If our desire is to serve God, and if we don't want to crawl through life defeated, it is essential for us to take the step of evaluation, without any reservations and with great honesty.

In the previous chapter I mentioned the Scripture in Hebrews 12 verse 1 where we are told that the Christian life is much like running a race. Thinking of a 100 metre dash for example, we can learn a great deal about focus by looking at the two most important rules to observe while running such a race. First: You must never look back, always remaining focused on the goal ahead; and secondly: You must be careful not to slow down or give up before crossing the finish line. (How comforting it is to know that, at times when we feel exhausted, unable to run any further, He will lift us up and carry us for a while.)

Victory only comes when we develop and maintain a right focus in life. We need to understand that we are drawn to that which we focus on. If we look to people, we will sooner or later be disappointed since we are all still flesh. And self-focus might just end in self-destruction. If our focus is to accumulate material possessions, we will find out that thieves might steal them, or inflation, rust and moths will eat them away. And if our focus is on the problems we face, they will get bigger and bigger, weighing us down and leaving us hopeless. The heavy winds of adversity often prevent us from maintaining a right focus in life, causing us to sink into the deep waters of discouragement. (*Matt.14:29,30)

When our focus truly becomes Jesus, His Word and His will–instead of our worldly ambitions,

*Matt.14:29,30: And when Peter was come down out of the ship, he walked on the water, to go to Jesus. But when he saw the wind boisterous, he was afraid; and beginning to sink, he cried, saying, Lord, save me.

our problems, our "self" or other people–He promises to give us a new and exciting reason for living, with a completely different perspective. To have my eyes fixed on Christ means that everything else in life, whether it is my family, my career or my ministry, must get in line behind me, not blocking my view, my focus on Him. The only thing in front of me should be God's Kingdom, which is found in Jesus. And as I seek His Kingdom first, following behind will be the necessary other stuff in life which He is adding. (*Matt.6:33)

*Matt.6:33: But seek ye first the kingdom of God, and his righteousness; and all these things shall be added unto you.

With our sights set on the Lord, He will help us develop the ability to look at all areas in life through His eyes, which ultimately leads to freedom and victory. Such a Christ-focused lifestyle, when combined with the power of faith, will enable us to accomplish the impossible.

At the beginning of this chapter, I made a statement: "That which we focus on in life gets bigger and bigger..."

Let me end with a Biblical example of a right focus, leading to victory:

Once there was a young man. He was always so focused on God, that the joy God gave him into his heart caused him to sing, praising Him all the time. And because of his total focus on the Lord, His greatness and His goodness, the Lord became bigger and bigger in his life. So much so, that even huge problems he was facing could only amount to the size of a shrimp compared to his God. He knew in his heart that if only he would stay focused, always walking close to the Lord, no problem in the whole world would be able to overcome him. One day he was faced with the biggest challenge so far in his life, even threatening to kill him. But because of his focus and the size of his

God, he had such confidence that the incredible challenge didn't seem much bigger than a little shrimp. He took out his sling, placed a smooth stone...

A Christ-focused lifestyle, when combined with the power of faith, will enable us to accomplish the impossible.

Chapter 6

The Bunji-Jump Effect

BEFORE WE FINALLY get into the exciting second part of the book, where we will see what the foundation for a joy-filled and victorious Christian life is, I need to address the problem that most of us have with "new beginnings".

As important as we know it is, starting over can be the hardest thing to do in life. To leave the past behind, which could mean having to break free, is easier said than done for most people. Whether it is the struggle with the memory of a hurtful experience that keeps haunting us, or an ugly, maybe even sinful, habit that we can't seem to get away from; or the realization that, if we keep going the way we have been we're going to end up totally burned out. Somewhere deep down inside we know that we should get out of the rut, that we need a change. Could it also be that one of the reasons for our frustration is that we got tired of our mediocre Christian walk? Maybe we have realized that our time here on earth is too short to be blindly wasted, and that we want to see the life-changing power of Jesus Christ become reality in our lives.

But the decision to follow Jesus wholeheartedly, and to go for the full package of everything He has to offer, is not an easy one, because it usually involves a dramatic change–maybe even a fresh start, a new beginning. If we allowed ourselves to dream of a new and exciting, meaningful walk with Jesus, free from all the heaviness that weighs us down, or even the dream of a calling, we would discover that there is much more to life than we thought. The security that we hoped to find in a safe and predictable lifestyle would turn out to be rather dull and boring, and the safest place on this earth might just be in the middle of a war zone, if the Lord has us there for His purpose. What if God really has a personalized and exciting plan for each one of us, something that goes beyond just making a living (*Jer.29:11-13)? Could it be that we don't have to live defeated and crushed forever by the painful event that happened to us in the past? Is it possible that our long-time dream to be a missionary, for example, a dream that we threw out because it seemed so unrealistic, was not so impossible after all (**Phil. 4:13)? As we begin to seek the Lord in prayer, open and ready for a change, this dream might just become reality one day.

Unfortunately, the first person we share our exciting new vision with is often a "yeah but" Christian. I'm sure we've all met one of them. This is the kind of person who is set in their ways, always playing safe, and always cautioning others why they shouldn't do anything out of the ordinary: "Yeah, but don't you think you're a little too old/young for the mission field?" "Yeah, but what about the house you wanted to rebuild?" "Yeah, but don't you feel responsible for your family?" "Yeah, but didn't you just get promoted?" "Yeah, but you don't even have a job..." "Yeah, but God also said..."

These people seem to have a gift of discouragement. Stepping out in faith and trusting God is not exactly their idea of a Christian lifestyle. If Jesus would happen to walk by and

*Jer.29:11-13: For I know the thoughts that I think toward you, saith the Lord, thoughts of peace, and not of evil, to give you an expected end. Then shall ye call upon me, and ye shall go and pray unto me, and I will hearken unto you. And ye shall seek me, and find me, when ye shall search for me with all your heart.

**Phil.4:13: I can do all things through Christ which strengtheneth me.

ask such a person to follow Him, the answer would be... you guessed it: "Yeah, but...; and believe me, their reasoning usually sounds very good. I'm just glad the disciples weren't like that, otherwise the Gospel would have spread only as far as Jerusalem.

"No really, what if God doesn't want me to change?" Sorry, but now we are obviously talking about a different god. The one and only true God from the Bible is in the "stretch to grow" and "break to renew" business, (no change, no growth!). His desire is to give us a new and exciting life, full of His wonderful purpose. But, in order to be able to appreciate and utilize the Lord's abundant blessings, we have to first be transformed, becoming compatible with what He wants to bless us with. The worst thing that could ever happen to us, after we've picked up our free ticket to Heaven, is to feel that we are doing just fine in our walk, or that we don't need any changes. We will only miss out on what God has in store.

So, the big question is: what causes us not to want to change, or to go for a fresh start, leaving the past behind, stepping out in faith, and trusting that He will provide all of our needs, just as He promises in His Word (*Phil.4:19)? There are different reasons why we despise change in our lives. The first one, as we just saw, is the pressure of other people's opinions, especially when they are family members or church leaders. The next one is our ancient, still-powerful enemy satan, and his workers of evil and discouragement. It doesn't take much for us to understand that it is not in his interest to see us go out and become missionaries, for example. I urge you to

*Phil.4:19: But my God shall supply all your need according to His riches in glory by Christ Jesus.

read the upcoming chapter on "the Spiritual War" where we will look at some of his motives and strategies.

Then there is the problem with apathy as mentioned in the previous chapter. We are too tired or too comfortable for a radical change. And the lack of understanding that God has great things in store for those who step out in faith, who love and follow Him wholeheartedly, doesn't help either (*Ps. 84:11).

Another thing which holds us back from doing as the disciples did, is our lack of self worth. "Who am I to think God has a calling for me? Just look at my life. Shouldn't I be content where I am? Why would God be interested in someone like me?" First of all, God is more than just interested in us. He made us. He says He knows every single hair we have, or have had (**Matt. 10:30). He made us very special (***Ps.139:14). We are His creation and He doesn't make any mistakes! We might still feel inadequate to be of any use to Him, but we need to remember that we do not depend on who we are in the first place. It is His love and grace, His righteousness and forgiveness, on which we stand. When we look at some of the great guys in the Bible, we see that they weren't perfect either, and yet God calls them His "friend", or "a man after my own heart"(****Acts 13:22).

The Lord chooses people differently than we do. He doesn't look at outward things such as education, popularity or looks. In fact His ways, most often, are completely the opposite of ours. Historians tell us that, in Biblical days, Shepherds for example, were the "outcasts" of society. They weren't even allowed to witness in

*Ps.84:11: For the Lord God is a sun and shield: the Lord will give grace and glory: no good thing will He withhold from them that walk uprightly.

**Matt. 10:30: But the very hairs of your head are all numbered.

***Ps.139:14: I will praise Thee; for I am fearfully and wonderfully made: Marvellous are Thy works...

****Acts 13:22: I have found David the son of Jesse, a man after mine own heart.

court, because their testimony was considered unreliable.

Interesting that God would choose a shepherd to become Israel's greatest King. And when the Messiah was born, He decided to share the good news with some shepherds first.

You see, when we think of what it takes to be used by God, it's not all that important who we are. What counts is that we deliberately decide to allow God to make us into the person He wants us to be. So, when it comes to a fresh start, it doesn't really matter where we are coming from, all that matters is where we are going in life. It is His continuous forgiveness that allows us to start over and over and over... Thank You Jesus!!

But there is a prerequisite for a fresh start. Before we can attempt to take a radical step of change, we must let go of everything that binds us or hinders us, to be free to move in the direction God wants us to. This is the letting go of our own agendas, our ideas and our burdens. Letting go of our past, our personal ambitions, and our own understanding, is the only way by which we can be genuinely open to His leading (*Prov.3:5). Here, I believe, we find one of the greatest problems when it comes to new beginnings; our inability to truly let go. We can not hang on to the past, even our hurts, in any way, while at the same time trying to have a fresh start. The stuff we hang on to, even small things, acts like a bunji cord. As we try to jump into God's open hands, we bounce right back into the old, unwanted lifestyle.

A sad example of the "bunji jump effect" is a person who was very dear to me. Her life was

*Prov.3:5: Trust in the Lord with all thine heart; and lean not unto thine own understanding.

characterized by some deeply hurting experiences. But because she kept hanging on to these painful events, they became part of her identity over the years. Had she truly let go of those hurtful memories, giving them all to Jesus and jumping wholeheartedly into His open hands, she would have been able to become free, filled with a new hope, experiencing the fullness of His love for her.

I certainly realize, that "letting go", for some people, is a huge step. And changes or accomplishments can not be achieved without overcoming a few obstacles. But isn't it worth to put up with some struggles and battles to gain the freedom He offers? When Moses prepared the way for the Israelites to go to the promised land, because of the problems they were facing, they would rather have stayed as slaves in Egypt than to be free.

Change isn't easy and a new beginning can be scary because of the factor of the unknown that lies ahead. But what choice is there, if we don't want to live as slaves under the things that oppress and weigh us down?! We must learn to trust God and His Word. His promise is to never leave us and to meet all our needs (*Heb. 13:5). He loves us more than we can ever imagine. We need to take that important step of faith. We must decide to let go of everything that keeps us from jumping, no bunji attached, into God's open arms. With His help, we will be able to cut off that which binds and hinders us from experiencing the freedom and the love Jesus wants each one of us to enjoy. Then He can take us and set us on a new and exciting path, where He walks closely with us, through the meaningful and fulfilling new life He gives us.

*Heb. 13:5: I will never leave thee, nor forsake thee.

"All changes, even the most longed for, have their
Melancholy, for what we leave behind is part of ourselves; we must die to one life before we can enter into
another."

Anatole France, French writer

Letting go of our past, our personal ambitions and our own understanding, is the only way by which we can be genuinely open to His leading.

Part II
More Than Conquerors

Chapter 7

Real Freedom – Life Under Grace

TO LIVE JOYFULLY AND VICTORIOUSLY, and to find strength and hope despite our circumstances, who wouldn't want that?! Walking through life with our heads and hearts lifted up, because of the confidence and the assurance we have in and through Jesus Christ. For so many of us, this seems to be an impossible dream. Frustrated and with guilt and condemnation weighing us down, we go through life heavily burdened and discouraged (*Rom.8:1). We try so hard to become a good Christian, to live more righteously and to have a better attitude toward others, but we just can't seem to get rid of those old, unholy habits. And when we're doing okay outwardly, we realize that our thought life isn't quite what it should be. We did all the things we felt God would be pleased to see us do, only to find out that, whenever we got one step ahead, two steps backwards followed. Why is it that, when we finally decide to roll up our sleeves and do God's work, we seem to end up in a dead end street of frustration? What else must we do in order to be a better Christian, so God can be pleased with us? The answer to our problem is quite simple and straightforward: No matter how sincerely we try, we can't do it! In fact, most of us would say, "It's not hard to live the Christian life, it's impossible." And here we find the secret to real freedom, which is to completely surrender everything in life to Jesus.

The world tries to convince us that freedom is independence, but this only leads to pride, when

*Rom. 8:1: There is therefore now no condemnation to them which are in Christ Jesus, who walk not after the flesh, but after the Spirit.

instead, real freedom is total dependence on God. This is the kind of freedom little children usually enjoy. As they completely depend on their parents, they do not worry about what to eat, what to wear, or where to sleep, and they never question their parents' love.

Let's go back and ask why it is so impossible for us to live the Christian life; and what hinders us from overcoming personal problems, holding us back from doing a mighty, victorious work of God? It is our "self", our flesh, our sinful nature. The fact that we are born into, and part of, a fallen world hinders us from becoming truly Christ-like. The things of Christ are not of this world, but we are. And our world and Christ's world are absolutely incompatible. His world with its laws and holy values is a supernatural, spiritual world. Our world with its laws and unholy values is a natural, physical world. But since we are now part of both worlds, we are torn, divided and weak. All the things we have been exposed to and conditioned with, in this world, are not automatically gone when we receive our free ticket to Heaven. To quote David Jeremiah: "Just because we are Christians now doesn't mean we have resigned from humanity." When we make the commitment to become a follower of Jesus Christ, we are still flesh and part of this world, and it's as if these two worlds within us begin to war against each other:

"For the flesh lusteth against the Spirit, and the Spirit against the flesh: and these are contrary the one to the other: so that ye cannot do the things that ye would"(Gal.5:17).

That is one reason why so many Christians become discouraged. When they accept Christ, they think that all of their problems are gone now. Instead, the battle has just begun.

For a lot of us, who became Christians later on in life, our fleshly nature had a huge head start. This means that all of these years we have been programmed and filled with the values, wisdom, and desires of this world; and we are still constantly contaminated by the things around us. Based on our fleshly nature, we now try to live the Christian life with our natural abilities. Therefore, the results of our "works in the flesh" are natural, weak and ineffective. Even though we have been saved by His grace and not of our own doing; our "doer" mentality and the fact that in our society we are conditioned to think that there are no free gifts of great value can easily cause us to try to earn God's love through the things we do (*Eph.2:8,9). We feel we have to do something or pay to deserve what we get, while our flesh tries to pull us under the legalistic carpet of scheduled prayer and devotions, church dress code and acceptable style of worship. How terrible it is when we slip back under the law, nullifying His cross, and the very blood that saved us (**Gal.2:21). Anything we do in the flesh feeds into the self-righteous pride-part of our sinful nature, pulling us away from God.

I believe the many obstacles we face in our Christian walk are there to constantly show us that we are weak, unable in our own strength, to live the life He calls us to live. It is our self-interest that hinders us from loving our neighbours the way we should, motivating us to try to impress others rather than to love them.

*Eph.2:8,9: For by grace are ye saved through faith; and that not of yourselves: it is the gift of God: Not of works, lest any man should boast.

**Gal.2:21: I do not frustrate the grace of God: for if righteousness come by the law, then Christ is dead in vain.

Only when we become free from our "self", or our self-focus, will we be free to love others and to see someone else's needs.

In God's Word, we find a strong indication of why it is essential for us to overcome our "flesh". As Paul wrote to the Galatians:

> "Now the works of the flesh are manifest, which are these; adultery, fornication, uncleanness, lasciviousness, idolatry, witchcraft, hatred, variance, emulations, wrath, strife, seditions, heresies, envying, murders, drunkenness, revellings, and such like"(Ga.5:19-21).

The only way by which we can overcome our weaknesses, is through the help of the One who did overcome this world – Jesus Christ. Denying Himself, He went to the cross for the sin of the whole world:

> ...but be of good cheer; I have overcome the world. To him that overcometh will I grant to sit with me in my throne, even as I also overcame, and am set down with my Father in His throne. He that hath an ear, let him hear what the Spirit saith unto the churches.(Jn.16:33; Rev.3:21)

This kind of genuine love can only grow in us when we become free from our "self". It is usually when our poverty and bankruptcy before God stares us in the face that we realize, we cannot live this Christian life in our own strength. And when we get tired of performing in order to please God and others; when we crawl out from under the legalistic carpet that is choking us; we have finally come to the place where our weakness becomes the key to the door of His strength, and where complete surrender is the only way to win this battle: "God, I can't live this Christian life, my weaknesses overwhelm me. I can't do it; I can't even fix my own problems. I don't have any answers anymore; I don't have any strength. I have tried so very hard but I can't do it. Lord Jesus I don't even want to do it anymore. Will You do it please? Will You live through me? Lord, I give my 'self', that which holds me captive, my own ambitions, all that I am, to You."

Ah, how freeing it is when we finally give up! When we run to Him for help and the heavy burden of living the perfect Christian life and trying to please God is lifted off of our hearts, and turned into a deep and honest desire to have an intimate relationship with our heavenly Father. How freeing, when we allow ourselves to become like little children with no more pretense, prerequisites and preconceived ideas (*Matt.19:14). And when we put our lives completely into our Father's hands, in awe of His greatness and embraced by His love, He enables us to dream and to see with our hearts, as we develop an openness and excitement about His world of miracles and wonders.

*Matt.19:14: But Jesus said, Suffer little children, and forbid them not, to come unto me: for of such is the kingdom of heaven.

Real freedom is the freedom from the prison of our "self", our worldliness and the cravings of the flesh. Only when we let go and put God in charge can we become more and more Christlike.

In Jesus we are free from self-consciousness, and from the insecurity and deception that causes us to feel that we have to earn or pay back what He has freely given. We are free from guilt and condemnation. It is the freedom from the passive position of our own captivity, that allows us to move into an active position, where we become free to be who God wants us to be. A practical illustration is when our freedom *from* greed is expressed in the freedom *to* give.

We are free to accept the fullness of His grace (*Rom.3:24), and free to sing and shout for joy (**Ps.5:11). We are free to dance like David danced (***2 Sam.6:14), and free to forgive and forget. We are free to love, and worship with our heart. Free to be a servant. Free to let go, through the confidence and strength He gives us. Free to allow others their freedom. Free to accept gifts, and free to sit at His feet like Mary did (****Lk.10:39). We are then free to be used by God in any way He wishes, and free to repent and to forgive ourselves. There will never be freedom where there is any form of un-forgiveness! We have a hard time loving someone if we don't even like ourselves. We can only be to someone else what we are to ourselves.

Jesus wants us to have this kind of freedom in our lives for the world to see and to desire. A life that is characterized by the freedom of living under the umbrella of His grace, without having to do anything other than to accept it, will cause us, with a sincere and thankful heart, to love Him with a different quality of love. When our relationship with Jesus Christ is based on this kind of love, it will produce a deep and honest desire in us to express our love in the things we do. Here we see a very important difference regarding our "works". The things we do out of love in freedom, initiated through our intimacy with Jesus Christ, are positive and fruitful, not heavy and burdensome, legalistic or religious. Now we don't *have* to please God anymore,

*Rom.3:24: Being justified freely by His grace through the redemption that is in Christ Jesus.

**Ps.5:11: But let all those that put their trust in Thee rejoice: let them ever shout for joy.

***2 Sam. 6:14: And David danced before the LORD with all his might.

****Lk.10:39: And she had a sister called Mary, which also sat at Jesus' feet, and heard His Word.

because we are free to accept His gift of grace. Rather, we *want to* please Him because of our gratitude and our love for Him. And I know that one way to please God is to acknowledge our dependence on Him in every aspect of our lives, humbling ourselves and saying, "Father I need you, I can't do it".

As we learn to look at life from a non-egocentric perspective, we begin to understand that our Christian walk never was and never will be about us in the first place. The sin that condemns us was committed by someone else in the Garden of Eden long before we were born. The penalty for that sin was paid for in full by someone else in Jerusalem long before we were born (*Rom. 5: 18,19). All we need is the freedom to accept His gift with a sincere and grateful heart.

*Rom. 5:18,19: Therefore as by the offence of one judgment came upon all men to condemnation; even so by the righteousness of One the free gift came upon all men unto justification of life.

When our self-focus is consumed by His love; when we become free to look past the walls of our "self"; it is then, that we are able to see someone else's brokenness. A free and open heart makes a good soil for love and joy to grow.

**Real freedom is
total dependence on God.**

Chapter 8

The Power Source – The Holy Spirit

ONCE WE HAVE DEVELOPED a wholesome and positive relationship with our Lord, based on love in freedom, truthfulness and openness, He can use us in a way we never imagined. Seeing that the Christian life is about Christ and not about us, He will soon become our main focus. The desire to intimately know the One who loved us so much that He gave His life for us, will draw us to meditate on His Word, and to pray like we've never prayed before.

But even though our relationship with Jesus is now built on a good foundation, we realize that we still don't have the power to do any of what He or His disciples did. We still struggle in our personal lives. How can we change the world around us, when we can't even conquer our own personal problems? Again, *we* can't do it. We need the Lord to do it in us, and through us. And how does He do it? How can we have victory over these problems? How can we do a mighty work of God in this world? We can do it, just like the disciples, through the power of His Holy Spirit.

In the Bible we read that before Jesus left, He told His disciples He would send a helper, the Holy Spirit (*Jn.14:26).

What a difference God's Spirit made in Peter's life, the one disciple Jesus called "the rock" (**Matt.16:18). Before Peter was Spirit filled, he wasn't quite that strong. Although he loved the Lord and believed in Him, his weakness in the flesh became evident when he denied Jesus

*Jn.14:26: But the Comforter, which is the Holy Ghost, whom the Father will send in my name, He shall teach you all things, and bring all things to your remembrance, whatsoever I have said unto you.

**Matt.16:18: And I say also unto thee, that thou art Peter, and upon this rock I will build my church; and the gates of hell shall not prevail against it.

*Matt.26:34: Jesus said unto him, Verily I say unto thee, that this night, before the cock crow, thou shalt deny me thrice.

three times, just as the Lord told him he would (*Matt.26:34). But after Peter received the Holy Spirit, the simple sermon that he preached was so anointed, so powerful, that three thousand people got saved, (let us remember that Peter was a fisherman, not a psychologist or motivational speaker). This wasn't the work of a man operating in his earthly flesh nature with all of its limitations and weaknesses. This was God's powerful Holy Spirit revealed through Peter.

It is in God's supernatural, spiritual world where we see power and victory. It was the supernatural, spiritual power at work, when Jesus and His disciples performed their miracles, even raising people from the dead. The supernatural overcame the natural. We need that kind of power, the power of His Holy Spirit in our lives and in the church today, to make a real difference and to change the world around us. The Bible tells us that, without His Spirit, we can't even understand God's Word (**1Cor.2:14). And the commandment to love our neighbours as we love ourselves is so much the opposite of who we are, that it is hardly possible for us, in our own strength, to fulfill it. In essence, we could say that the Christian life, with all of its values, is "out of this world", and that is exactly where our help must come from.

**1Cor.2:14: But the natural man receiveth not the things of the Spirit of God: for they are foolishness unto him: neither can he know them, because they are Spiritually discerned.

Before I go any further on the subject of God's Holy Spirit, I want to say that I am well aware of the fact that this is a very controversial topic. But because of the key role the Holy Spirit plays in the victory of the Christian church, I cannot stress enough the importance of being open-minded; and if necessary, to rethink our position.

Many believers have neglected the fact that we need the Holy Spirit to do a mighty work of God in the weakness of our sinful flesh nature. If anyone would have been able to do God's work without this Helper, it would have been Jesus' disciples. But, as we all know, they did what they did only because of His Holy Spirit. They knew that they would not be able to do anything without Him, and Jesus certainly knew that, too. Just try to imagine the disciples as they argued with Jesus regarding His Spirit: "That's really nice of you Lord, but we don't think we need this Helper. Thanks, but no thanks." Dare anyone argue with Jesus? When the Lord says that we need a helper to do His work, we can be one hundred percent sure we need that Helper!

Nevertheless, there are all kinds of reasons why people don't want to deal with the issue at all. I believe one of them is that the "unseen world" has been mystified. In our hi-tech, computerized western culture, we are very used to living by the slogan "seeing is believing". It seems very hard for an intellectual, pragmatic, scientific-realist to comprehend the existence of the spiritual realm. And again, too much head knowledge is not very helpful, as it quenches our imagination. For many people it is also scary to think that there is a whole other world all around us, a world we can't see and therefore don't have any control over. This is quite interesting when we realize that, for the disciples, the realm of spirits was a day-to-day, very real, meat-and-potato issue. They were dealing with evil spirits all the time (*Acts 5:16).

I personally think that the lack of knowledge and understanding of spiritual matters is one of

*Acts 5:16: There came also a multitude out of the cities round about unto Jerusalem, bringing sick folks, and them which were vexed with unclean spirits: and they were healed every one.

the main problems in the church today. The disciples were well aware of the "unseen world" because Jesus taught them all about it.

Another huge problem we find when we question why people neglect the Holy Spirit, is in recognizing one of the spiritual gifts. This of course is the gift of speaking in other tongues. (Leslie Flynn mentions 19 gifts in his book.) I personally know far too many people who have been turned away from God's Holy Spirit because someone told them that, if they don't have the gift of speaking in tongues, they are not really spiritual. In other words, something is wrong with you if you don't possess a spiritual language. What is really disturbing is that some people, because of the pressure of church leaders, learned to speak in tongues by listening carefully to their fellow Christians, (so much for the God-given gift).

There are three points which will clarify things. First of all, the ability to speak in another tongue is a gift, and not something we have earned because we're so extra special. Just as salvation is absolutely undeserved, so also are any of the gifts of the Holy Spirit. God gives as He pleases, when He pleases. We do not earn His gifts through our performance as Christians. In fact, our righteousness is as filthy rags to Him (*Is.64: 6).

*Is.64:6: But we are all as an unclean thing, and all our righteousnesses are as filthy rags...

Secondly, if the gift of tongues is such an important measure of a person's spirituality, why is it that Jesus Himself didn't stress it? Why doesn't the Bible tell us that, immediately after Jesus received the Holy Spirit, He began to speak in other tongues?

And thirdly, when we look at what Paul wrote to the Corinthian church, it appears that to have the gift of a spiritual language is not as imperative as some people would like to think. Not everyone possessed the gift and there is something more important anyway:

> "Are all apostles? Are all prophets? Are all teachers? Are all workers of miracles? Have all the gifts of healing? Do all speak with tongues? Do all interpret? But covet earnestly the best gifts: and yet show I unto you a more excellent way. Though I speak with the tongues of men and of angels, and have not charity (love), I am become as sounding brass, or a tinkling cymbal. And though I have the gift of prophecy, and understand all mysteries, and all knowledge; and though I have all faith, so that I could remove mountains, and have not charity, I am nothing. And though I bestow all my goods to feed the poor, and though I give my body to be burned, and have not charity, it profiteth me nothing"(1 Cor.12: 29-31; 13: 1-3).

> "He that speaketh in an unknown tongue edifieth himself; but he that prophesieth edifieth the church. I would that ye all spake with tongues, but rather that ye prophesied: for greater is he that prophesieth than he that speaketh with tongues, except he interpret, that the church may receive edifying. Now, brethren, if I come unto you speaking with tongues, what shall I profit you, except I shall speak to you either by revelation, or by knowledge, or by prophesying, or by doctrine?"(1 Cor.14: 4-6)

So, for those of us who speak in tongues, let us be ever so humble and grateful for His gift. And let us use it to glorify Him, and not to make those who don't have it feel un-spiritual. To those who do not have a spiritual language, please remember that those of us who did receive this gift from God, did nothing to earn or deserve it.

Just because you don't have it, doesn't mean you are worth less than someone who speaks in tongues. Keep asking the Lord for it, and eagerly desire His precious gifts, but do it for the right reasons, (may the spirits of pride and legalism, who create disunity in the body of Christ, flee from His church and never return!)

There are many rumours out there regarding the Holy Spirit and these, so-called manifestations. I am sure that a lot of people in Jesus' days didn't go to Him because of some wild rumours the Pharisees were spreading about Him. What a way to miss out on the most incredible, life giving teachings! Preconceived ideas and personal opinions are also hardly helpful in trying to find truth. Even to this day, most people in Israel are still waiting for the Messiah. Jesus just didn't come the way they thought He would come. How terrible when our insecurities or our pride and stubbornness create walls around us, when we can't see the opportunities on the other side because we have made up our mind.

Understanding that the victory of the church comes from God through His Spirit, (just like salvation also came from God through Jesus Christ) it is only logical that satan will try to distort and discourage anything to do with the Holy Ghost. He even has the power to do it in the church. Just because we've had an experience regarding God's Spirit that we didn't expect or understand, should not lead us to blindly reject it. Whenever we encounter something that we can't seem to comprehend, instead of being quick to judge, we should be quick to pray for insight and discernment:

"For my thoughts are not your thoughts, neither are your ways my ways, saith the Lord. For as the heavens are higher than the earth, so are my ways higher than your ways, and my thoughts than your thoughts"(Is.55:8,9).

Satan of course would like to see us powerless. Trying to fight him without the Holy Spirit is like fighting with a straw against a roaring lion. The devil is a spiritual, invisible being and so are his demons. There is a good reason why God tells us in His Word that our battle is not against flesh and blood–a physical battle–but it is a spiritual battle against the powers and the principalities of a dark world (*Eph.6:10-12). And it is not by might and not by our own power that we can fight this battle, but by His Spirit alone (**Zec. 4:6).

Still, there are many people today who believe that the Holy Spirit is not for us, that he was given as a helper to Jesus' disciples only. Let me show you that this view cannot be true according to Scripture. In the book of Acts chapter 19 we read that, when Paul came to Ephesus, he found some disciples who were believers, but had not yet received the Holy Spirit. This is obviously not talking about Jesus' disciples. The next thing we read is that Paul put his hands on them and they received God's Spirit. In Galatians 5:16 we are told to live by the Spirit. In Ephesians 5:18,19 and 6:18, Paul commands us to be filled with the Holy Ghost, to sing spiritual songs, and to always pray in the Spirit. Jesus tells us, as we read in John 6:63, that our flesh counts for nothing. It is the Spirit who gives life. And in John 4:23,24 He says, that as true worshipers we will worship the Father in Spirit and truth. If this

*Eph.6:10-12: Finally, my brethren, be strong in the Lord, and in the power of His might. Put on the whole armour of God, that ye may be able to stand against the wiles of the devil. For we wrestle not against flesh and blood, but against principalities, against powers, against the rulers of the darkness of this world, against spiritual wickedness in high places.

**Zec.4:6: Then he answered and spake unto me, saying, This is the Word of the Lord unto Zerubbabel, saying; Not by might, nor by power, but by my Spirit, saith the Lord of hosts.

doesn't convince us of the fact that we need His Holy Spirit, hopefully the Scripture in Gal. 5:22,23, will. Here we are told that "the fruit of the Spirit is love, joy, peace, long-suffering, gentleness, goodness, faith, meekness, temperance: against such, there is no law". The fruit of the Spirit is..., and not of our own doing. We can not produce this kind of fruit without Him. He does it, and so He gets the glory! Realizing that fruit doesn't grow well in a dark and stuffy prison, it becomes evident that our freedom is a key ingredient in a fruitful Christian life. If we suppress the Holy Spirit with a close-minded, legalistic attitude by trying to squeeze Him into a box of religious ideas, He can not unfold or bloom and breathe.

Now, let us take a final look at the four fundamental reasons why we need God's Holy Spirit, why we don't have a choice.

Reason No. 1

The Christian life, without any help, is impossible for us to live, because its laws and values come from a different world: The supernatural, spiritual, Holy world of God. Jesus sent His helper because He knows we need Him.

Reason No. 2

In His Word, the Lord commands us to be filled with the Holy Spirit and to eagerly desire spiritual gifts (*Eph.5:18; **1Cor.14:1).

Reason No. 3

We can not have Jesus in our lives, receiving His salvation, without also accepting His Spirit. God the Father, Jesus and the Holy Spirit are one. We can't separate them (***1 Jn.5:7).

Reason No. 4

The Bible tells us that there is a battle going on

*Eph.5:18: And be not drunk with wine, wherein is excess; but be filled with the Spirit.

**1Cor.14:1: Follow after charity, and desire Spiritual gifts.

***1Jn.5:7: For there are Three that bear record in heaven, the Father, the Word, and the Holy Ghost: and these Three are One.

in the spiritual realm. And although we are still flesh, living in a natural, physical world, as Christians we have become part of this battle. (see Eph.6: 10-12)

What it really all comes down to, is the fact that God is the centre of everything! It took God to create us. It took His Son Jesus to save us, and it takes His Holy Spirit to help us accomplish that which He has planned for each one of us individually, and for the church in general. And since the Lord is really doing it all, He gets the full glory for everything, so that no man can ever boast!

What a blessing–and how freeing it is–when God basically offers to do it all for us. This brings us right back to the previous chapter where we talked about freedom. As long as we are slaves under the cravings of our fleshly nature, we are driven to become self-sufficient instead of God-dependent.

Part of our freedom in Christ is the freedom to make personal decisions. Again, our relationship with the Lord is based on love in freedom. We are not robots without any choice. This is the quality of our relationship. We want to love Him, we want to serve Him, and we want to be available to Him. Yes, the Lord is basically doing it all, but He allows us to play an active role in His plans.

From the beginning of mankind, God invited man to participate in His ventures, when He put Adam in charge of the Garden of Eden. So the question is what our part is in God's "business" for today? Is there anything we can, or should, do? There certainly is. The Holy Spirit came as helper and not as someone who completely takes over. And as little as it seems, most of us find it very hard to do our part. Our Christian walk involves constant decision-making, followed by the appropriate actions.

When we look at Paul's command to be filled with the Holy Ghost, it makes sense to think that we can't be filled unless we are empty first. Which means, we need to deliberately empty ourselves of all the "stuff" that preoccupies us: our own ambitions, our own understanding, goals and desires. As long as we are full of our "self", will there not be much room to be filled with His Spirit. In other words, we must decrease so that Jesus can increase in our lives; we need to make room for Him– an active decision on our part. Next, we need to read and meditate on His Word (*Ps.119:148;**1Tim.4:15), and we must pray without ceasing (***1Th.5:17), making ourselves available, ready at all times for Him to use us. Last but not least, we should eagerly desire spiritual gifts just as we are told in God's Word.

Earlier we looked at the fruits of the Holy Spirit, the attitudes that He will produce in our lives when He is present and in control. Now we want to look at specific abilities and skills He gives us in order to accomplish our unique, individual calling and certain tasks. Let us always be mindful of the fact that these wonderful things God gives us, beginning with our salvation, the good fruit He produces in us, and the free gifts He offers, are not our own personal accomplishments!

Eagerly desire, or in modern English, "be hot for" spiritual gifts, obviously means that we need to actively get involved before any gifts

*Ps.119:148: Mine eyes prevent the night watches, that I might meditate in Thy Word.

**1Tim.4:15: Meditate upon these things; give thyself wholly to them; that thy profiting may appear to all.

***1Th.5:17: Pray without ceasing.

will be delivered. Let's think about that for a moment. If we would want to give someone an expensive present, we most likely would make sure that the person will appreciate our gift and not ignore it. We wouldn't want to waste it on someone who is not even interested. It would be like throwing pearls before swine (*Matt.7:6). And we certainly wouldn't force it on someone who is not asking for it. Realizing that God's gifts are more precious and priceless than anything we could ever dream of, it only makes sense that He doesn't waste them on people who are not interested. I believe the bottom line is we receive no gifts without passion, or without being "hot" about them!

*Matt.7:6: Give not that which is Holy unto the dogs, neither cast ye your pearls before swine, lest they trample them under their feet, and turn again and rend you.

Let us take a closer look at some basics. It is essential for us to know the difference between spiritual gifts and natural abilities. When the Holy Spirit comes to help us accomplish His will, He comes with a giant toolbox. These tools are His spiritual gifts. According to His plan and purpose, and combined with our eagerness and passion to serve Him, He then hands out His free gifts–His tools–to help us do the job effectively.(Remember, He gives when He pleases. His timing is perfect!) These jobs, or tasks, can be individually very different. For some it might be a lifelong calling into ministry and for others it might just be a onetime event in a Sunday morning church service. In other words, you could have the calling to be a full-time evangelist, needing the gift of evangelism, whereas someone else's job is to deliver a word of prophecy to the congregation next Sunday.

Our natural abilities are very different from spiritual gifts, as they have to do with the way

God made us, our personality and our physical and mental capability. As God gives us different jobs, He usually combines the two. Our natural ability might be to speak well in front of a large crowd of people; but when He adds His gift of evangelism, incredible things can happen. In essence, it is the spiritual gift that brings the powerful supernatural aspect into the picture. As Christians, we all have a general calling: the call to witness, the call to worship our Lord, etc. Some have a specific calling, but not everyone is called to be a full-time evangelist or worship leader. We all should witness but not all will have the gift of evangelism.

The nice thing about gifts is that they take away from guilt and competition. We are not running our own show any more. It is Jesus, His Holy Spirit, working through us. All we have to do is be open and available, eagerly desire His gifts and carefully obey His Word. When Jesus' Holy Spirit is in control of our lives, He will produce good fruit. With His supernatural power we will be able to overcome all kinds of obstacles and challenges. He is our comforter and friend (*Jn.14:16). And when He equips us with His gifts, we will be able to do a mighty work of God for the glory of the Father. As Jesus taught His disciples, so will His Holy Spirit teach us. Leading us to maturity, He will show us useful and important things we must know. We will learn, for example, that grace can only be understood on the basis of the fear of the Lord. A fear that doesn't oppress and choke us, but a fear that says, "I respect You, my Father, because You are my Creator. You are almighty in Your power, and I know You love me". He will teach us to discern

*Jn.14:16: And I will pray the Father, and He shall give you another Comforter, that He may abide with you for ever.

and to understand circumstances. We will learn to look at life through His eyes, enabled to see more and more of "the big picture". As a friend, He will also help us to see when we fall short, and how to make things right. Like an artist who carves a beautiful sculpture out of a raw and rough material, so the Holy Spirit, when He chisels away at us, wants to bring out the beautiful picture of Christ-likeness.

We could also see the Holy Spirit as a master surgeon. He cuts deep as He works on our hearts, our attitudes and our perspective. And His work produces lasting changes of a great quality. The evidence of the presence of the Holy Spirit in a person's life is therefore mainly seen in that person's day-to-day lifestyle, and not so much in the possible manifestations during a church service. As mature Christians we should be more interested in His lasting, life-changing power and love than in a Holy Ghost buzz or a "good feeling" on a Sunday morning. (The icing on top of a cake is sweet and tasty, but it wouldn't be much without the cake.)

When we think of the supernatural power of God's Spirit in the context of a ministry, we realize the incredible potential there is, provided He is in control. Again, we need to decrease so that He can increase! I believe we don't have to invent great ideas to make church fun and exciting. When the anointing of the Holy Spirit is there, He will draw the people and they will not be able to stay away. Jesus didn't have to provide free coffee and doughnuts in order to get people to come to His meetings. The people will be thirsting for His presence, and the days where a pastor feels he has to apologize for going a little overtime will be gone. I cannot imagine anybody apologizing for what God is doing anyway (*Gal.1:10).

*Gal.1:10: For do I now persuade men, or God? Or do I seek to please men? For if I yet pleased men, I should not be the servant of Christ.

As much as Jesus and the Heavenly Father are welcome in our churches, oftentimes the Holy Spirit is kept outside the door because He is feared to be too radical and unpredictable. He might change the order of the service, or even cause things to happen that are strange and improper according to the rules we have established. The desire to create a safe and predictable environment at church has caused many leaders to quench the very source of freedom and victory–God's Holy Spirit. Even though there might be growth in numbers, if we don't see the changes and empowerment that the Lord promises to us in His Word, we must question whether the Holy Spirit is in the "driver's seat". Only when God's Spirit is given free reign will He be able to use us in the most incredible ways:

> "And these signs shall follow them that believe; In my Name shall they cast out devils; they shall speak with new tongues; They shall take up serpents; and if they drink any deadly thing, it shall not hurt them; they shall lay hands on the sick, and they shall recover" (Mk.16:17,18).

So far it seems that, in most parts of the world, the church is like a sleeping giant. As His people, we need to come to a greater understanding of the power we have in, and through, God's helper, and then utilize that power (**2 Cor.10:4). The secret to doing a mighty work of God in this world lies in God Himself (***Rom.8:31,32; 37-39). Therefore: The effectiveness of a ministry is not

**2Cor.10:4: For the weapons of our warfare are not carnal, but mighty through God to the pulling down of strong holds.

measured by the number of books we've read or how many seminars we've attended, not even by the amount of prayer prayed on behalf of the ministry, but only by the powerful, life-changing, presence of God's Holy Spirit. His power is unlimited. He can do what we can't do. We must let go and let God..., becoming equipped, empowered and authorized through His Holy Spirit...; the harvest is ready!

In the following chapter we will talk about our adversary who deceives, discourages and destroys: satan, the fallen angel of God. We will learn who our enemy is, and how we have been deceived in many ways. This will hopefully lead to an even greater understanding of why we can not possibly live our Christian lives without God's helper in control of everything.

***Rom.8:31,32; 37-39: What shall we then say to these things? If God be for us, who can be against us? He that spared not His own Son, but delivered Him up for us all, how shall He not with Him also freely give us all things? Nay, in all these things we are more than conquerors through Him that loved us. For I am persuaded, that neither death, nor life, nor angels, nor principalities, nor powers, nor things present, nor things to come, nor height, nor depth, nor any other creature, shall be able to separate us from the love of God, which is in Christ Jesus our Lord.

**God is the centre of every-
thing and it takes His Holy
Spirit to do His work!**

Chapter 9

Spiritual War – A Reality

WHAT IS REALITY? For some people reality is the hard facts of their bank account numbers, and for others, the upcoming promotion in their profession. Yet others think of the alarm clock going off in the morning as traumatic reality, or a broken leg that cuts down a person's mobility. For most people that which is perceived as reality, has to do with a natural, physical matter. In this chapter we will look again at a very different reality; the reality of the "unseen world", the supernatural, spiritual realm; but this time we will look at the dark side of it.

When we study God's Word we quickly discover that our physical, natural world, in its mortality, is very weak and bound by many limitations. The eternal, supernatural, spiritual realm, is where the powers are, (where "the real stuff" is happening).

While living in a natural physical world, as Christians we are part of the scheme of things in the "unseen world". (This is hard to imagine for someone who grew up in a visual society overflowing with magazines, videos and TV, etc.) But even though we are somehow connected to both (the physical and the spiritual world), we don't have any impact on the spirit realm with our natural abilities. And when we see our position in the context of a spiritual battle, we easily understand that our carnal weapons of the flesh are useless in such a war.

Let us look once more at the Scripture in Ephesians 6 verses 10 to 12:

"Finally, my brethren, be strong in the Lord, and in the power of His might. Put on the whole armour of God, that ye may be able to stand against the wiles of the devil. For we wrestle not against flesh and blood, but against principalities, against powers, against the rulers of the darkness of this world, against spiritual wickedness in high places"(Eph.6:10-12).

The battle we are involved in is not against flesh and blood, not a physical battle against people, but a battle against the devil and his helpers. We are told to be strong in the Lord, not leaning on our own strength. It is His power and might we depend on!

When it comes to fighting a battle, any battle, it is of strategic importance to know who our enemy is, what he is capable of, and what his motives and tactics are. In the book of Ezekiel, we find a clear description of our adversary before his fall:

"Thou sealest up the sum, full of wisdom, and perfect in beauty. Thou hast been in Eden the garden of God; every precious stone was thy covering, the sardius, topaz, and the diamond, the beryl, the onyx, and the jasper, the sapphire, the emerald, and the carbuncle, and gold: the workmanship of thy tabrets and of thy pipes was prepared in thee in the day that thou wast created. Thou art the anointed cherub that covereth; and I have set thee so: thou wast upon the holy mountain of God; thou hast walked up and down in the midst of the stones of fire. Thou wast perfect in thy ways from the day that thou wast created, till iniquity was found in thee" (Ez.28: 12-15).

Satan was a cherub, an anointed angel. He is most beautiful and full of wisdom; the perfect angel of God. And as God's angel, he is a created being just like all the other angels. This is a very important truth for us to understand. Many Christians view satan as God's equal except that he operates in the realm of evil. This, of course, is absolutely impossible. A creation can never, in any way, be equal to the creator! And we can never measure satan up against his Creator God. It would be like comparing a house with its architect.

When we elevate satan to a position where we compare him with the God of the universe, we give him far too much credit, which can be dangerous. We might end up fearing him above God, especially since the fear of the Lord is not very popular these days.

However, as a special angel satan was powerful enough to deceive one-third of all the angels in Heaven to follow him (*Rev.12:4). (According to some scholars, the number of angels who joined satan's "club" was in the millions.) These are his helpers, known as demons. It is obvious that one of the devil's outstanding abilities is to deceive. If satan was able to trick even God's angels, how much easier it must be for him to deceive ordinary human beings, particularly when they are unprotected and unaware of his powerful influence.

*Rev.12:4 And his tail drew the third part of the stars of heaven, and did cast them to the earth: and the dragon stood before the woman which was ready to be delivered, for to devour her child as soon as it was born.

The following Scriptures in Isaiah and Ezekiel tell us about satan's fall and why he was kicked out of heaven:

"How art thou fallen from heaven, O Lucifer, son of the morning! How art thou cut down to the ground, which didst weaken the nations! For thou hast said in thine heart, I will ascend into heaven, I will exalt my throne above the stars of God: I will sit also upon the mount of the congregation, in the sides of the north: I will

ascend above the heights of the clouds; I will be like the most High"(Is.14:12-14).

"Thine heart was lifted up because of thy beauty, thou hast corrupted thy wisdom by reason of thy brightness" (Ez.28:17).

Lucifer, the angel of light, fell because of his pride, culminating in self-exaltation. He thought he could be just as great as God Himself. What a good example of how pride can cause the complete loss of a reasonable perspective.

Satan and his demonic helpers were thrown onto the earth. That is where they are still today, roaming around like lions, waiting to devour us:

"Be sober, be vigilant; because your adversary the devil, as a roaring lion, walketh about, seeking whom he may devour"(1 Pet. 5:8).

Here we see the devil's primary motive. He wants to devour, to destroy us, because we are God's most precious creation. And as Christ's followers, who worship the Lord, we are promised a place in heaven where the devil wanted to be king. Satan must be fuming! He was dreaming of the whole universe worshipping him; instead, he was thrown out and we were allowed in.

But not only did the Lord kick the devil out of heaven, He also prepared a special place for him in the future:

"And the devil that deceived them was cast into the lake of fire and brimstone, where the beast and the false prophet are, and shall be tormented day and night for ever and ever"(Rev.20:10).

Satan knows where he is going in the end, and he wants to pay God back for it by taking as many people with him as possible. He knows that his days are numbered, but he also knows how it grieves the Father's compassionate and loving heart to see even one single soul lost.

Now that we have talked about satan's motive for his works of evil, let us look at Scripture verses clearly showing that satan is really with us here on earth:

> "And the great dragon was cast out, that old serpent, called the devil, and satan, which deceiveth the whole world: he was cast out into the earth, and his angels were cast out with him"(Rev.12:9).
>
> "And the Lord said unto satan, Whence comest thou? Then satan answered the Lord, and said, From going to and fro in the earth, and from walking up and down in it"(Job1:7).

There are many more Scriptures indicating the devil's ugly presence on earth. And when we look around in the world of today, we can clearly see his evil power at work. Apart from the fact that he is, most likely, quite nervous about his future, I guess we could say that he's alive and well.

An important question, often asked, is how satan can have any influence in a person's life. The following Scriptures give us a definite answer:

> "But He (Jesus) turned, and said unto Peter, Get thee behind me, satan: thou art an offence unto me: for thou savourest not the things that be of God, but those that be of men"(Matt.16:23).

> "And when He had dipped the sop, He gave it to Judas
> Iscariot, the son of Simon. And after the sop satan
> entered into him"(Jn.13:27).
> "But Peter said, Ananias, why hath satan filled thine
> heart to lie to the Holy Ghost, and to keep back part of
> the price of the land (Acts 5:3)?"
> "And that they may recover themselves out of the
> snare of the devil, who are taken captive by him at his
> will"(2 Tim.2:26).
> "Wherefore we would have come unto you, even I Paul,
> once and again; but satan hindered us"(1Th.2:18).

Satan's evil spirit is able to influence, and also enter into a person. Interesting that Peter didn't even realize that he was used by the devil. This shows that a person without God's counsellor, the Holy Spirit, whom Peter hadn't received yet, is so much more susceptible to becoming a victim of the devil, without even knowing it.

The Scripture in 2 Cor. 12: 7 reveals that satan's accomplices are also actively involved in his business:

> "And lest I should be exalted above measure through
> the abundance of the revelations, there was given to
> me a thorn in the flesh, the messenger of satan to buf-
> fet me, lest I should be exalted above measure."

Satan uses all kinds of different tactics, and his devices and strategies have become more and more sophisticated, yet there are many people today who believe that we shouldn't blame the devil for every bad thing that happens. The truth is that satan, although very powerful, is not omnipotent, all-powerful, or omnipresent, (always present); only God is. Satan cannot be at two different places at the same time, and neither does he have the power to do whatever he wants. However, as much as we should be careful not to give him too much credit, exalting him above his limitations, it is critical for us never to underestimate satan's power and influence. The Bible clearly warns us about the devil's schemes:

> "Lest satan should get an advantage of us: for we are not ignorant of his devices"(2Cor.2:11).
> "But I fear, lest by any means, as the serpent beguiled Eve through his subtlety, so your minds should be corrupted from the simplicity that is in Christ"(2Cor.11:3).
> "Woe to the inhabiters of the earth and of the sea! for the devil is come down unto you, having great wrath, because he knoweth that he hath but a short time.
> And the dragon was wroth with the woman, and went to make war with the remnant of her seed, which keep the commandments of God, and have the testimony of Jesus Christ"(Rev.12:12,17).

The devil has come to make war against Christ's followers, and he is mad like a wounded animal, aware that his end is coming soon. In the second chapter of the book of Revelation, the writer mentions the depth of satan. After all, he was God's special angel— which makes him very powerful.

It is not always easy for us to determine what is devilish deception and what is plainly human error, sinful nature, or just bad choice. The fact that satan and his demons are invisible, spiritual beings leads us very quickly to the conclusion that we can not possibly identify and fight these evil forces without any outside help. It takes "spiritual eyes" to see the enemy, and it takes "spiritual weapons" in order to fight and to win such a battle. It is therefore imperative for us to have the Holy Spirit in our lives, not only to convict us of our own sin, but also to counsel us regarding our choices, and to reveal to us when we are attacked or deceived by satan or his helpers. The Holy Spirit is the only available source who has the power to expose and to defeat the devil and his angels. Only spirit can fight spirit, and the war must be fought and won in the spirit first, before we will see any results in the natural. We must hand our lives over to Him completely, in order to find protection, and to attain freedom and victory as individuals, and for the church in general.

But as usual, God wants to work with us, and we are commanded to do our part. This is our protection when we obey His Word:

> "Wherefore take unto you the whole armour of God, that ye may be able to withstand in the evil day, and having done all, to stand. Stand therefore, having your loins girt about with truth, and having on the breastplate of righteousness. And your feet shod with the preparation of the gospel of peace; Above all, taking the shield of faith, wherewith ye shall be able to quench all the fiery darts of the wicked. And take the helmet of salvation, and the sword of the Spirit, which is the Word of God: Praying always with all prayer and supplication in the Spirit, and watching thereunto with all perseverance and supplication for all saints..."(Eph.6:13-18).
> "Submit yourselves therefore to God. Resist the devil, and he will flee from you" (Js.4:7).

Disobedience goes hand in hand with destruction. The first example of this truth is found at the beginning of mankind in the Garden of Eden.

Now, let us take a closer look at how satan works his evil deeds in today's world. There are a few important things we should always keep in mind when we try to analyze the devil's presence. The first one is that his main goal is to make war against Christians. But the Bible also mentions that he deceives the whole world, which of course affects believers as much as non-believers (*Rev.12:9,17). Although many have had a physical encounter with demons, satan and his angels usually operate on a spiritual level, using and manipulating people for their wicked purpose. We are not fighting against human beings, but rather against the spiritual force who is influencing those who come against us.

One more significant characteristic to remember about satan is that he is full of wisdom (**Ez.28:12). Being as smart as he is, he knows God's Word better than any Bible scholar, and his ways are very subtle and deceitful.

When we look at the history of North America, we can see that our nations were founded on the basis of Godly standards and ideals, thus giving us a strong Christian heritage. To this day in no other part of the world will we find more people who openly profess their testimony of Jesus Christ. (As previously mentioned, satan's number one business here on earth is to eliminate those who *"have the testimony of Jesus Christ"* (Rev.12:12,17). Let us also remember that the American nation is still the only real supporter of Israel (God's chosen people), and that some of the largest missions and Christian aid organizations are based here in North America. All of this could very well explain the devils' special inter-

*Rev.12:9: And the great dragon was cast out, that old serpent, called the devil, and satan, which deceiveth the whole world: he was cast out into the earth, and his angels were cast out with him.

**Ez. 28:12: Thou sealest up the sum, full of wisdom, and perfect in beauty.

est in the destruction of our culture. It shouldn't come as a surprise to us that the spirit of anti-American sentiment is spreading fast, while the increasing isolation and pressure against Israel is a strong indication that satan has also kindled a fresh fire of anti-Semitism in many nations.

It seems to me the devil works with some basic principles. Satan, although his personal crowd is getting bigger, knows that not everyone on this earth will worship him outright. If he can get us to worship anything else other than God, he has done his job. And he also encourages sin which, of course, is contrary to God's Word. What God says we shouldn't do is exactly what satan will try to deceive people into. For example, in His Word the Lord warns us not to drink too much alcohol which would lead to all kinds of troubles:

> "And be not drunk with wine, wherein is excess; but be filled with the Spirit"(Eph.5:18). "Wine is a mocker, strong drink is raging: and whosoever is deceived thereby is not wise"(Prov.20:1).

Each year, in North America alone, thousands of people die from alcoholism or associated complications. And the cost to medically treat the millions of people who suffer from substance abuse and related medical problems, goes into the hundreds of millions of dollars; not to mention the growing number of babies born with fetal alcohol syndrome, and the horrific impact alcohol has on families.

God's moral standards and wholesome values are eroding fast in our modern society. Prisons are bursting at the seams, and the news about violence in schools has become part of our daily bread. Never before have there been so many broken homes with an ever-increasing divorce rate, and the cases of sexually transmitted diseases, as well as HIV and AIDS, have reached epidemic proportions. The stuff children are exposed to these days, through magazines, movies, and video games, would have made most people sick to their stomachs only twenty years ago. (If you want to destroy a nation, just get hold of its future.) Meanwhile, the killing of unborn babies is celebrated as victory in the battle for women's rights, and the voices of certain minority groups are getting louder and louder, while their rights become more and more extended.

The question we need to ask is: are people just too ignorant in their self-destructive behaviour, or are we rather seeing a global form of devilish deception taking place? I personally believe that, ever since the Bible and prayer were banished from our schools, that which somewhat protected our society was thrown out the window. (Do you wonder who was behind that decision?) Under the mantle of human rights and personal freedom, and driven by an evil love of money, our so-called civilized nations have been handed over to the most decadent forms of immorality and violence. The fact that people at the helm of our nations profess to work for the welfare of the country, but are unable to see how our society is progressively deteriorating, should be seen as an indication that a higher power is at work behind the scene. Blinding and deceiving are most definitely satan's specialties.

There are basically two main kinds of deception satan seems to use: direct or personal deception, and indirect or general, global deception. Both usually work hand in hand. Since the devil's power and manpower is somewhat limited, he uses people in central, influential positions to do, and to spread, his dirty work. Satan may use personal deception on a famous artist or filmmaker, for example. He misleads such a prominent person to portray sexual immorality as acceptable. This may also become a form of indirect or global deception of his or her audience.

The recognition of certain values and standards in our society is greatly influenced by the lifestyles of some people with immense popularity. Idolized by many, they easily become role models. Their persuasive power goes as far as "dictating" to millions of young people what kind of clothes to wear in order to be cool and acceptable. (We talked earlier about how our insecurities, the longing to feel good about ourselves, to be accepted and to belong, make us very vulnerable.)

The strong messages that are coming from popular magazines and movies have a tremendous sociological impact. Today's media, with its brain-washing power, is obviously not only used by well-meaning business people advertising their products.

The student and free love movements of the sixties found a lot of their fuel in the messages of popular music groups during that time. And the news of young people committing suicide after listening to a famous rock band's invitation "to get out of here", shows just how far the influence of people in key positions in our society can go, (especially when there is a supernatural, spiritual force involved).

When we take a look at the political arena, we easily recognize satan's evil, manipulative spirit at work. A prime example is Adolf Hitler. Who else, other than satan, could have given Hitler such a charismatic, hypnotic power, deceiving millions of Germans to follow him in his odious quest to annihilate God's chosen people, and to become world leader?!

Many political decisions and changes have indirectly affected Christians, and the church as a whole, over the years. But satan's war against God's people has become more open and aggressive these days. According to a missionary who recently spoke at our church, a religious fundamentalist group in Indonesia is literally hunting down Christians who have hidden in the jungles of some islands.

Every year, hundreds of thousands of believers around the world are persecuted for their faith, many of whom are killed. The pressure on the Christian church is continually increasing as biblical end-time prophecy is finding its fulfillment.

The devil works in big and in small ways. He is quite imaginative. At times he comes with a screaming brutality, outright violently like a wolf in hot pursuit of his prey. But he also comes like a gentleman with a friendly, convincing smile on his face, his hand stretched out toward us.

There are numerous examples of satan's fingerprints on our society. One is that he was clever enough to turn our Lord's birthday celebration into a most lucrative commercial event.

But the commercialization of something that belongs to God isn't really all that new, seeing how the Pharisees and others turned the temple in Jerusalem into a marketplace (*Mk.11: 15-17).

*Mk.11:15-17: And Jesus went into the temple, and began to cast out them that sold and bought in the temple... And He taught, saying unto them, Is it not written, my house shall be called of all nations the house of prayer? But ye have made it a den of thieves.

I would like to take a look now at how the devil works in the lives of Christians and also in the church. A general observation is that satan is a great copycat. He is constantly trying to imitate God's voice and God's ways; but, of course, that which the Lord intends for good, satan uses for evil. In the previous chapter we talked about how God combines our natural abilities, our personality and certain talents, with His Spiritual Gifts to empower us for His purpose. Satan, in the same way, will use a person's natural abilities and possible influential position, to do his work. We saw earlier how a musical talent can either be used to drive people into a horrible act of suicide, or to lift them up by creating an atmosphere of praise and worship unto God. When the Lord uses the gentle and sensitive personality of a compassionate counselor, He may bring healing to a broken heart. Satan will also exploit certain personalities. Someone who is predominantly melancholy for example, makes a great target for his attack. Dispatching a demonic spirit of negativism and hopelessness, satan might try to drive such a person into a major depression. Here we can see that the main battlefield in our war against the devil is a person's mind, and that it is essentially important for us to constantly "fill our heads" with God's powerful Word of truth:

*"But I see another law in my members, warring
against the law of my mind, and bringing me into captivity to the law of sin which is in my members"
(Rom.7:23).*

*"...casting down imaginations, and every high thing
that exalteth itself against the knowledge of God, and
bringing into captivity every thought to the obedience
of Christ" (2Cor.10:5).*

The devil works with a very poisonous formula. He uses "DDT", which, in this case, is
Deception, Discouragement, and Temptation.
Since the Garden of Eden, he is still trying to
trick us with the same old story, telling us that
"God didn't really mean that", and that we
shouldn't take His Word literally–it needs to be
"interpreted."

The following is a list of some of the devil's
most commonly used phrases when he "talks"
to us:

"His grace covers everything you do. God is so
loving, He understands your feelings. He knows
that you are weak, that you can't help it. He
wants you to be happy, and it doesn't really matter what you do anyway, because there is no
more sin. Jesus paid the price for it all. Just go
ahead and do it..."

"How could you even think of doing such a
thing! God can never accept you."

"Your wife never really loved you."

"Your husband never really cared about you."

"God obviously didn't want this marriage."

"God will take care of her and the kids, so don't
worry."

"As long as you go to church, God will be
pleased, no matter what."

"Don't be so religious, you don't have to go to

church every Sunday."

"Why should you have to put money in the offering? God knows you can't even afford a holiday."

"Look how much you give to the church; you're going to sit right next to Jesus in Heaven."

"God doesn't want you to change, He made you the way you are."

"You don't have to pray all the time, God knows everything anyway."

"Why would God want to pay attention to someone like you? Don't waste your time praying."

"God entrusted this ministry to you, so you better take charge and make sure it works well."

"Some people in your congregation are not happy with your sermons. You are way too critical. Remember you are here to serve people."

"Everybody liked Jesus. Be careful not to step on anybodies toes."

"If this was from God, people wouldn't be offended."

"The success of your ministry, depends on how hard you work at it."

"God wants you to focus on people, find out what they like and don't like."

"Be careful with all that Holy Spirit stuff. Remember God likes order in the church."

"The only way you can get closer to God is when you please Him. Work at it!"

"Who do you think you are? Don't even dream of spiritual gifts."

"What is wrong with you? You can't even manage to have regular devotions."

"You blew it again this week; don't even bother going to church."

"You are so un-spiritual. Just compare yourself with him or her."

"Your past is written all over your forehead. I wouldn't be so sure that God loves someone like you."

"You'll never be able to please God, just look at your dirty past."

"What makes you think God could use you? Just be content that you are saved."

"You still don't speak in tongues. You'll never be really spiritual."

"Better be quiet in the church and in your home-group. You don't even know what you're talking about."

"What a nice woman; she really understands you. Too bad your marriage isn't the greatest. You and your wife just don't match."

"Come on, a little flirt doesn't hurt anybody."

"Don't even try worshipping the Lord, you sound awful."

"Can't you see the financial advantage of this job offer? Even if you can't go to your home-group and prayer-meeting any more, you'll be able to give so much more money to the church."

This was just a sample of the "DDT" that satan tries to poison our minds with on a regular basis. Since he most often uses other people to work on us, another good example, when it comes to temptation, would be the new secretary in your office who is so broke, that she can only afford to buy clothes to cover one-third of her body. Keeping in mind that satan knows very well that your marriage is going through a valley at the moment, it is not at all surprising he involved himself in the hiring process.

Then there is the charismatic preacher who deceives a whole congregation by presenting a false grace message. Insinuating that it is religious and old-fashioned to talk about the fear of the Lord, and that modern Christians have to be open and willing to compromise, satan might use such a person for the watering down of God's standards and values. A well-known Bible teacher once suggested that, if we were to find the devil in the church, instead of trying to find him hiding under the back pew, we would more likely see him behind the pulpit.

But how can it be that a preacher can be deceived and then deceive his congregation? First of all, we need to see that a person, although employed in God's business, is still human. That is why we should never blindly follow anyone other than Jesus. Secondly, the more we get involved in the Lord's work, the more we become a thorn in satan's eye, which will put us at a higher risk of being attacked. There are many "fallen angels" in the church today. Leaders who at some point have lost their focus on the goal, which is to glorify God, and Him alone. (It's amazing how all things might work together for evil for those who have lost their sense of clear direction.)

We need to realize that we as a congregation play a vital role in the picture. If we don't take ownership of our ministries by actively participating in the strengthening of their foundations through prayer and intersession, and the encouragement of our leaders, we open the door for satan to attack. The worst thing that could happen to a preacher, who like most of us has a problem with pride, is that his congregation blindly adores him, while putting him up on a pedestal. Instead of thanking the Lord for using this man, praying for him and keeping him accountable, they feed right into his pride problem. It could be said that satan is the most accomplished psychologist. He knows exactly where we are weak and vulnerable. And although he may not be able to know our future or read our minds, he has studied our behaviour long enough, and thoroughly enough, to predetermine how we will react when he pushes certain "buttons" in our lives. Let us again remember that to obey God's Word is our protection. The Bible clearly commands us to uphold our leaders (*2 Cor.1:11; **Heb.13:18), and the Bible's warning, regarding false prophets and teachers, shows how we need to be on guard (***2 Pe.2:1).

In the final part of this chapter we will look at the three most successful strategies satan applies in his battle against God's people. The first one he uses is to try to prevent us from building a close, intimate relationship with the Lord. Such a relationship, while giving us a strong foundation in Him, would lead us to maturity as Christians. Standing firmly grounded on His truth, and led by His Holy Spirit, we then would be able to discern and uncover the ways of the devil.

Through the distraction of an overly-busy lifestyle, and filled with worldly ambitions and materialistic desires, we easily lose our focus on the one important thing in life—Jesus Christ. When our relationship with the Lord is shallow, our roots are also not very deep. The first storm that satan brings against us could easily knock our marriages, our families and our faith down

*2Cor.1:11: Ye also helping together by prayer for us.

**Heb.13:18: Pray for us: for we trust we have a good conscience, in all things willing to live honestly.

***2Pe.2:1: But there were false prophets also among the people, even as there shall be false teachers among you.

into the pit of discouragement. It is our foundation that determines whether or not we will be able to stand in the end.

Another, most common and extremely successful strategy the devil uses is the deception of believers through a legalistic, religious spirit. If satan can't keep us from believing in Jesus Christ, he at least will try to limit our effectiveness as Christians by luring us into the "place of religiousness", which is surrounded by walls. These walls, as a major part of the deception plan, are there to give us a sense of protection. Our insecurities, and the drive to be in a position of control, easily make us susceptible to falling into the trap of being religious rather than relational in our pursuit of Christ. It is much easier and less demanding to accept and practice a "form" of Christianity than to diligently and patiently work at the development of a meaningful relationship with Jesus Christ. (Let me state clearly that the traditions and religious routines and rituals found in the church are not at all restricted to particular age groups or denominations.)

The most significant difference between a personal relationship with Jesus and a religious attitude is that a relationship is like a living, breathing organism; it is dynamic, and always subject to change and growth; whereas religion is lifeless, cold and dry. In God's Word the Lord uses the example of a vine and its branches to describe our desired relationship with Him:

"I am the true vine... Abide in me, and I in you. As the branch cannot bear fruit of itself, except it abide in the vine; no more can ye, except ye abide in me. I am the

vine, ye are the branches: He that abideth in me, and I in him, the same bringeth forth much fruit: for without me ye can do nothing" (Jn.15:1,4,5).

Just like a garden needs to be well-watered and kept free from the weeds that easily come and choke and destroy, so also a relationship, in order for it to be alive, to be fruitful and to grow, must be nurtured; it requires a person's willingness to work at it, to be considerate and patient, and to be open for changes. Only when we are continually open to learn and grow, and willing to adjust, will we be able to bear fruit. And as we abide in Him, may we never despise the necessary times of being pruned.

The walls of religion, seemingly there to protect us, do not allow us to be free and open for changes, to venture out, and to explore by faith what God has in store for His people. It is most often a religious spirit that hinders us from recognizing a sovereign move of God. The most profound example of the deceiving power of religion is seen in the lives of the Pharisees who were unable to recognize Jesus as the long-awaited Messiah. Disconnected from the vine, religion cannot bear fruit and eventually dries up.

When we look at the teaching and the application of Biblical truths, we could say that religion proclaims and applies God's Word without God's presence. His Word only comes alive in its powerful, supernatural dimension through the presence and the anointing of the Holy Spirit. Just as Adam, after the Lord had created him from the dust of the earth, was yet without life, so also God's Word, unless He breathes life into it, is not very effective. It is God's spiritual anointing that makes the Bible a book unlike any other book.

Now let us look at the third and very efficient weapon satan uses against us; the weakening of the church through disunity. In the Scriptures we read how unity gives strength and comfort; and an army that is well trained, standing together as one man, can not easily be defeated (*Ps.133:1; **Ecc.4:12).

*Ps.133:1: Behold, how good and how pleasant it is for brethren to dwell together in unity!

**Ecc.4:12: And if one prevail against him, two shall withstand him; and a three-fold cord is not quickly broken.

Satan is shooting his bitter and poisonous arrows of gossip, un-forgiveness, jealousy, pride and prejudice at the church, keeping us from standing strong and united. The time has come for the body of Christ to turn from a passive position of complacency, compromise and defeat, to the active position of an army. An army that will stand up for what is right, proclaiming His truth and Lordship. An army that will not be pushed back any further! Are we willing to fight for His Name's sake? Are we ready to kick the demon of disunity out of our churches? Are we willing to confront the spirit of religion? What does it take for God's people to say, "Enough is enough? We will not give up any more ground! We will not stand by any longer, watching God's Holy Name and standards pushed into the dirt! We will fight for His glory and the precious Name of our Lord Jesus Christ!"

***Lk.10:19: Behold, I give unto you power to tread on serpents and scorpions, and over all the power of the enemy: and nothing shall by any means hurt you.

But there is no victory without a battle; and a battle is always active, and never passive. God provides us with the strength of a giant. In His Word the Lord promises us victory over the devil and his demons (***Lk.10:19). With the help and the counsel of His Spirit, we will be able to identify those areas where satan has deceived us.

When we cover ourselves with "the full armour of God", we are protected against the devil's attacks (*Is.54:17). As the Holy Spirit equips us with weapons that are not carnal, but mighty through our Lord, we will be enabled to conquer that which the devil has stolen: our marriages, our children, our land (**2 Cor.10:4).

Whole cities in Africa and South America have already been delivered from many years of terrible oppression and bondage. Where there used to be witchcraft, crime, prostitution, and prisons, a spirit of praise and worship has taken over.

With God's help we are able to recognize where there are strongholds and then tear them down, (greater is the Holy Spirit in us, than the devil, who is in the world (***1 Jn.4:4).

What are the actual weapons we must use in order to be able to drive the devil out of town? It all begins with our foundation. We cannot fight effectively if we are standing on shaky ground. We might just get pushed over. Here is a Biblical example of what can happen if we go into battle without the right preparation:

> "Then certain of the vagabond Jews, exorcists, took upon them to call over them which had evil spirits in the Name of the Lord Jesus, saying, We adjure you by Jesus whom Paul preacheth. And there were seven sons of one Sceva, a Jew, and chief of the priests, which did so. And the evil spirit answered and said, Jesus I know, and Paul I know; but who are ye? And the man in whom the evil spirit was leaped on them, and overcame them, and prevailed against them, so that they led out of that house naked and wounded" (Ac.19:13-16).

*Is.54:17: No weapon that is formed against thee shall prosper.

**2Cor.10:4: For the weapons of our warfare are not carnal, but mighty through God to the pulling down of strong holds.

***1Jn.4:4: Ye are of God, little children, and have overcome them: because greater is He that is in you, than he that is in the world.

These guys, it seems, did what they did out of a wrong motive–which allowed the demon to prevail. Before we can successfully fight against satan or his angels, we need to build a strong base–a rock-solid foundation, which is a true, intimate relationship with Jesus Christ. Anything we do as Christians can only be fruitful and effective if it is birthed out of such intimacy with our Lord. When we are driven by a deep passion for our Saviour and filled with His Holy Spirit, we then will be able to use the anointed weapons of praise, prayer, faith and His Word to overpower the enemy.

"Think not that I am come to send peace on earth: I came not to send peace, but a sword." (Matt.10:34)

Only spirit can fight spirit;
and the war must be fought and
won in the spirit first before we will
see any results in the natural.

Chapter 10

The Powerful Lifestyle of Worship

TO WORSHIP GOD is much more than just singing and praising Him through music. Worship is a lifestyle, and there are many different ways in which we can worship our Creator. The old English mother-term of the word "worship" is the word "worth-ship", which means to assign correct worth to something or someone. When we worship the Lord, we proclaim that He is worthy.

Anything we do that will glorify Jesus Christ can be seen as an act of worship: when we get up in the morning, thanking Him for a safe night and a new day; when we show an attitude of gratitude for all that He gives and has given; when we walk by faith according to His Word, and when we obey His commands; when we make time to talk with Him in prayer, and when we fast; when we use the gifts and talents He has given us to glorify Him; when we give to the ministries that He has ordained; when we honour His Name by portraying Christ-likeness in the way we relate with others; when we praise Him in song; and when we acknowledge that He is the author and giver of every good thing; all of these are acts of our worship unto God. In Romans 12:1, the apostle Paul sums it all up by asking us to present our bodies as a living sacrifice.

A true revelation of what the Lord has done for us, and what we have been saved from, should naturally cause us to extend our worship into all areas of our lives. Jesus did not limit His sacrifice for us in any way; He gave all that He could give.

It is easy to see that our worship is expressed through our "giving", the giving of our time, our money and our talents. Anything we either hold back from Him, or use in a selfish manner, creates a distance between us and the Son, which causes our hearts to grow cold. We could say that our level of intimacy with Jesus Christ is reflected in the way we give. The closer we get to the source of life, the more we are drawn to worship the One who is the source.

For us to give to the Lord is a little bit like the way children give to their parents. When Dad's birthday is coming up they ask him for money so they can buy him a present. In other words, everything we have comes either directly or indirectly from God. First of all, He gave us life or we wouldn't be here. And then He gave us our hands and brain, allowing us to work and earn a living. So when we give money to a ministry, for example, we only give back from that which He enabled us to generate. The same goes for our creative talents: our ability to worship Him through music, dance, drama, painting, and poetry. All we can do basically, is give back to the Lord that which He has given to us.

We need to understand that our worship is based on a decision we make. Just as love is a decision rather than a feeling, so also are our acts of worship. Sometimes our decision to worship the Lord may collide with certain man-made rules. Mary, at the risk of getting into trouble, preferred to sit at Jesus' feet instead of following the rules of hospitality by helping Martha in the kitchen (*Lk.10:40-42).

*Lk.10:40-42: But Martha was cumbered about much serving, and came to Him, and said, Lord, dost Thou not care that my sister hath left me to serve alone? Bid her therefore that she help me. And Jesus answered and said unto her, Martha, Martha, thou art careful and troubled about many things. But one thing is needful: and Mary hath chosen that good part, which shall not be taken away from her.

When King David decided to dance before the Ark, he knew that this was a very unusual thing for a King to do . But to worship the Lord, at any cost, was more important to David than to follow the rules of a King's courtesy, or to be concerned about what the people might say (*2Sam.6:21,22). Wanting to please God rather than man, including ourselves, is one of the pillars of our worship:

*2Sam.6:21,22: And David said unto Michal, It was before the Lord, which chose me before thy father, and before all his house, to appoint me ruler over the people of the Lord, over Israel: therefore will I play before the Lord. And I will yet be more vile than thus, and will be base in mine own sight: and of the maidservants which thou hast spoken of, of them shall I be had in honour.

"For do I now persuade men, or God, or do I seek to please men? For if I yet pleased men, I should not be the servant of Christ"(Gal.1:10).

David and Mary were criticized for what they did. This is an example to us, that whatever we attempt to do for God may cause some form of discouragement or resistance to arise. The motives behind our acts of worship are purified in the crucible of evolving, resisting factors. It is easy to praise God when things are going well for us, and it is easy to give out of our abundance. How much greater the reward for those who worship Him in spite of their circumstances (**Lk.21:1-4; ***Heb.13:15).

**Lk.21:1-4: And He looked up, and saw the rich men casting their gifts into the treasury. And He saw also a certain poor widow casting in thither two mites. And He said, Of a truth I say unto you, that this poor widow hath cast in more than they all: For all these have of their abundance cast in unto the offerings of God: but she of her penury hath cast in all the living that she had.

But our worship, in order to be pleasing and acceptable to God, has to meet a certain standard, for whatever we do must be honest and straight from the heart. Jesus doesn't look at outward things the way we do. He isn't very much impressed with the wrapping of a gift, no matter how beautiful it may be:

***Heb.13:15: "...therefore let us offer the sacrifice of praise to God continually..."

"These people draweth nigh unto me with their mouth, and honoureth me with their lips; but their heart is far from me. But in vain they do worship me, teaching for doctrines the commandments of men"(Matt.15:8,9).

The Father loves it when we give freely and cheerfully of our resources, but the greatest act of worship is to fully commit our hearts to Him. And when our worship becomes a heart matter, it will also become our lifestyle.

There are four things that happen when we worship. The first is that, by worshipping Jesus with all of our resources and in all kinds of ways, we acknowledge His rightful place as Lord of our lives. Secondly, true worship is an eternal investment into God's Kingdom, as we build treasures in Heaven. Thirdly, worship from the heart is the key that opens the door to the room of God's many blessings. And, last but not least, worship–specifically in the form of music– is one of the most powerful weapons in our warfare against satan and his demonic forces.

When we establish God's throne in our lives by surrendering all to Jesus, we automatically begin to grind away at the devil's kingdom. We could say that all acts of worship are also acts of warfare against satan and his angels. However, the one form of worship, that seems to be most efficient in the battle against our enemy, is music. This could very well be attributed to the fact that musical worship has a significant place in the heavenly realm (*Rev.14:2,3).

It also appears that satan, equipped with some built-in pipes, seems to have been created for the very purpose of worship:

*Rev.14:2,3: And I heard a voice from heaven, as the voice of many waters, and as the voice of a great thunder: and I heard the voice of harpers harping with their harps: And they sung as it were a new song before the throne.

"The workmanship of thy tabrets and of thy pipes was prepared in thee in the day that thou wast created" (Ez.28:13).

Could it be that, for the devil, worship music has become a very painful experience, ever since he refused to play his pipes unto the Most High God?

Furthermore, the language of music is universal and therefore a powerful unifying element amongst all Christians worldwide. Many believers also feel that music, in its uniqueness, communicates on a deeper, more intimate level than the spoken word.

When Jesus Christ is celebrated, when we exalt Him and proclaim His truth, we create an atmosphere of "Heaven on Earth"; and when the Lord's presence fills a place of praise and worship, the devil will have a hard time breathing (*Matt.18:20).

*Matt.18:20: For where two or three are gathered together in my name, there am I in the midst of them.

It is not at all surprising that there are many reports of people who have been physically and emotionally healed during worship services. Evil spirits will flee in the presence of true worship unto God, and even prison doors will fly open, and chains fall off, through the power of praise:

"And it came to pass, when the evil spirit from God was upon Saul, that David took an harp, and played with his hand: so Saul was refreshed, and was well, and the evil spirit departed from him"(1Sam.16:23).
"And at midnight Paul and Silas prayed, and sang praises unto God: and the prisoners heard them. And suddenly there was a great earthquake, so that the foundations of the prison were shaken: and immediately all the doors were opened, and every one's bands were loosed"(Ac.16:25,26).

One of the most outstanding examples of what worship can accomplish, is found in 2 Chronicles 20:

> "O our God, wilt Thou not judge them? For we have no
> might against this great company that cometh against
> us; neither know we what to do: but our eyes are upon
> Thee. And Jehoshaphat bowed his head with his face to
> the ground: and all Judah and the inhabitants of
> Jerusalem fell before the Lord, worshipping the Lord.
> And when they began to sing and to praise, the Lord
> set ambushments against the children of Ammon,
> Moab, and mount Seir, which were come against Judah;
> and they were smitten."

The Lord could have destroyed these aggressors while the King and his people were looking on, twiddling their thumbs. Instead, God's people became actively involved in the battle by worshipping. Let us remember that God works through people in order to accomplish His will. When David played his harp the evil spirit had to flee because of God's spiritual anointing on the music. Our musical worship in the natural, when charged with spiritual energy, is transformed into warfare in the spirit realm. The weapons Jehoshaphat and his people used were singing and praising. When we sing a song of praise, or strike a guitar or drum as an act of true worship from the heart, I believe the Lord spiritually empowers and then directs these drum strokes as heavy blows into the face of the enemy:

> "Blessed be the Lord my strength, which teacheth my
> hands to war, and my fingers to fight" (Ps.144:1).

As Christ's representatives we are also His spokespeople. We could say that He is speaking through us against our adversary. There is a tremendous strength in the words we sing or speak: *"Death and life are in the power of the tongue"* (Prov.18:21). When we shout an empowered, spiritually charged shout of praise, the enemy is beaten down: *"For through the voice of the Lord shall the Assyrian be beaten down, which smote with a rod"*(Is.30:31).

Jesus, being tempted in the desert, defeated satan with *"...the sword of the Spirit, which is the Word of God"* (Eph.6:17).

God is not personally coming down from heaven to fight against the evil one; instead He is using us with our instruments as weapons to drive out devils and demons:

> *"David took an harp and played with his hand, and the evil spirit departed"*(1Sam.16:23)
> *"And in every place where the grounded staff shall pass, which the Lord shall lay upon him, it shall be with tabrets and harps: and in battles of shaking will He fight with it"*(Is.30:32).

The Biblical accounts, where the power of musical worship is described, only emphasize how Jesus delights in the praises of His people (*Ps.149:3,4). As we draw near to God in worship, He will draw near to us (**Js.4:8). And when we praise His Holy Name and declare His Lordship over all the earth, the enemy has to flee.

God created our world with many different sounds. His creation of melody and rhythm are reflected in every singing bird, and in every beating heart. But since the gift of music is such an enjoyable one, we must be very careful not to fall into the trap of becoming worshipers of music, or of those whom God has gifted with a musical talent. Band performances that draw our attention to the quality of musicianship and

*Ps.149:3,4: Let them praise His Name in the dance: let them sing praises unto Him with the timbrel and harp. For the Lord taketh pleasure in His people.

**Js.4:8: Draw nigh to God, and He will draw nigh to you.

sound equipment, and the regular Sunday routine of a five song "sing along" session, will hardly invite God's glory to fall on a congregation

We should always remember that the Lord, first of all, listens to a man's heart rather than to his voice. He is not impressed with a song, no matter how beautiful and professional it may sound, when the heart is cold and distant.

May our praise and worship reflect a deep longing in us as we are desperately thirsty for His presence; and may we strive to delight ourselves in Him, and Him alone!

When Jesus Christ is the centre of our lives, the true reality of our relationship with Him will be a visibly different and contagious lifestyle of worship; a continuous celebration of His everlasting love.

The many different signs and sounds of true worship are the outward expressions of a soft and hungry heart, deeply touched and changed forever by God's glory.

The closer we get to the source of life, the more we are drawn to worship the One who is the source.

Chapter 11

Faith – Nothing Goes Without It!

NEED A FAITH-LIFT? I guess most of us do at times. Sooner or later we will all be enrolled in God's faith-fitness program. We could say that faith is like a muscle. The more it is exercised and the more intensely, the stronger it gets.

According to God's Word, there is nothing of great value in our Christian walk that could be done without faith at the core. It begins with our salvation: *"For by grace are ye saved through faith"* (Eph.2:8). Since we didn't actually see with our own eyes how Jesus died and rose again, we can only accept by faith, and through the revelation of the Holy Spirit, that His Word is true. Faith is the only possible path that leads to God, for we will never be able to fully perceive and understand His ways (*Is.55: 8,9). When it comes to our relationship with the Lord, we are told that we cannot find His approval without faith: *"But without faith it is impossible to please Him"* (Heb.11:6). In fact, faith should be our daily bread, the standard for Christian living: *"Now the just shall live by faith"* (Heb.10:38). It is our faith, the uncompromising trust in God and His Word, that creates the desired quality of a father-child relationship.

The Bible gives us many examples of incredible tasks that could only be accomplished through the power of faith. It was faith that enabled Noah to find the strength and perseverance to build the ark (**Heb.11:7). The chemical which hardened the water beneath Peter's feet and allowed him to walk on it was faith.

*Is.55: 8,9: For my thoughts are not your thoughts, neither are your ways my ways, saith the Lord. For as the heavens are higher than the earth, so are my ways higher than your ways, and my thoughts than your thoughts.

**Heb.11:7: By faith Noah, being warned of God of things not seen as yet, moved with fear, prepared an ark to the saving of his house; by the which he condemned the world, and became heir of the righteousness which is by faith.

*Matt.14:29: And when Peter was come down out of the ship, he walked on the water, to go to Jesus.

(*Matt.14:29). Then there was Abraham's wife, Sarah:

> "Through faith also Sarah herself received strength to conceive seed, and was delivered of a child when she was past age, because she judged Him faithful who had promised "(Heb.11:11).

The combination of God's promise and Sarah's faith achieved the impossible. Solid walls come crumbling down when faith is applied, and even the water of the Red Sea goes out of its way to accommodate those who walk by faith:

> "By faith the walls of Jericho fell down, after they were compassed about seven days. By faith they passed through the Red Sea as by dry land: which the Egyptians assaying to do were drowned"(Heb.11:30,29).

Over and over we read how Jesus criticized the disciples for not trusting Him and His Word. Looking at our own lives, we easily recognize that our lack of faith is generally a sign of unbelief. The root cause for unbelief is, most often, an insufficient heart-knowledge of God and His unconditional love for us. We usually only trust someone we know. Consequently, the deeper our relationship with Jesus becomes, the more our faith will increase, which is the foundation for "the peace of God, which passeth all understanding" (Phil.4:7).

It doesn't take much for us to discover that, in order to please God, to find peace, and to be able to do "big things", we must have faith.

Faith, put simply, is "the substance of things hoped for, the evidence of things not seen" (Heb.11:1).

Faith is what turns a God-given desire, or even an impossible dream, into a realistic goal.

Now the question is where our Christian faith comes from: *"Jesus the author and finisher of our faith"* (Heb.12:2). Again, there is really not much we can do without Him:

> *"He that abideth in me, and I in him, the same bringeth forth much fruit: for without me ye can do nothing"* (Jn.15:5).

Faith is also closely connected to God's Word: *"So then faith cometh by hearing, and hearing by the Word of God"* (Rom.10:17). The prophet Elijah, for example, states that he only did what the Lord told him to do:

> *"Elijah the prophet came near, and said, Lord God of Abraham, Isaac, and of Israel, let it be known this day that Thou art God in Israel, and that I am Thy servant, and that I have done all these things at Thy Word"* (1 Kings18:36).

Biblical faith will always have its roots in God, and it can never be viewed disconnected from Him and His Word. Genuine Christian faith is based on two things: Personal revelation or some form of evidence. Faith that doesn't have any foundation on which it operates is wishful thinking, rather than faith. An incorrect conception of faith has even caused some believers to lose their lives. We've probably all heard of incidences where people were told that if only they had enough faith, they would be healed of their terminal illness. The tragedy is that, these people, in order to show a great amount of faith, never went to see a doctor for a medical treatment. We can not drum up faith, and we need to be very careful that faith in itself doesn't become our motivation. As much as we must desire faith, it should never be our main focus, taking the place of God.

When we look at those who came to Jesus Christ in order to be healed from their diseases, we see that their faith had a strong foundation. First of all, they had seen or heard that this man was truly able to miraculously cure people; and secondly, they knew that He was also willing to do it. When they came to Him, their faith was based on evidence. Peter's faith, allowing him to climb out of his boat, was also based on evidence combined with the Lord's Word. Not only did he see Jesus walk on water, which showed him that it is possible to do so, but he also confirmed with Him that it was okay to step out onto the lake: "Come on Peter, you can do it, trust my Word!"

Then there was Noah. Being warned by God of things not yet seen, he trusted God's Word and built a ship in a land where it had never rained before. His faith was based on God's revelation, and so was Sarah's. The Lord, through His Word, revealed to Abraham and Sarah that He would give them a child. Their faith was the confidence and trust that God would keep His promise; this is the faith that pleases Him, when we don't doubt or question His Word:

"Let us hold fast the profession of our faith without wavering; for He is faithful that promised (Heb.10:23).

The real issue concerning our faith is the question where the things we hope for, the things not yet seen, originate. Who, or what, motivates us to do what we do? Who is behind our desires? Are they inspired by our flesh, or sparked by our enemy? Are they God's idea? This brings us right back to the most fundamental and critical subject regarding our Christian walk, our relationship with Jesus Christ. Is it shallow and shaky, or deep and strong? Is it religious or personal?

Our faith to believe and trust that God is going to do a certain thing is worth nothing, if that thing we hope for wasn't born out of an intimate relationship with Jesus, and somehow inspired by Him. As the author of our faith, God must also be the author of our dreams and desires. Here we find the prerequisite for all of God's promises in the Bible. His promises are always based on His will! The Lord blesses His goals, not ours. When our desires absolutely correspond with His will, He will give us the faith to know that He is going to do whatever we ask in His Name (*1Jn. 3:21,22). Jesus will provide us with the strength we need to pursue the dreams He gives us. We could say that faith is not only the energy that turns a God-inspired dream, or desire, into a realistic goal; but it also is the fuel that keeps us going on the path to its achievement.

Now, let us look at two different levels of faith. The first level is the general Christian faith. This is the kind of faith at work when we get saved, or when we trust the Lord to meet our daily needs, according to the promise in His Word. Then there is the level of what I like to call power-faith which, like all the other spiritual gifts, comes with a specific bestowed ability (**1Cor.12:8,9). It is the big and extraordinary

*1Jn.3:21,22: Beloved, if our heart condemn us not, then have we confidence toward God. And whatsoever we ask, we receive of Him, because we keep His commandments, and do those things that are pleasing in His sight.

**1Cor.12:8,9: For to one is given by the Spirit the word of wisdom; to another the word of knowledge by the same Spirit; To another faith by the same Spirit.

122 Awakening The Sleeping Giant

tasks that require such a gift, (big things need bigger faith.) I can see that tearing down the walls of Jericho called for such power-faith. The foundation for Joshua's faith was revelation. God revealed to him what was about to happen, and He also gave Joshua clear instructions regarding the realization of His plan. Here we can see that obedience, as well as works, play an important role in the overall faith picture:

> "What doth it profit, my brethren, though a man say he hath faith, and have not works? Even so faith, if it hath not works, is dead, being alone. Ye see then how that by works a man is justified, and not by faith only" (Js.2:14,17,24).

The most incredible example of how obedience and works are closely connected with our faith is found in Abraham's life:

> "Was not Abraham our father justified by works, when he had offered Isaac his son upon the altar? Seest thou how faith wrought with his works, and by works was faith made perfect? And the Scripture was fulfilled which saith, Abraham believed God, and it was imputed unto him for righteousness: and he was called the Friend of God"(Js.2:21-23).

Let me try to make it a little more practical for us today: in His Word the Lord promises to meet all of our needs, but He also commands us to work. By faith we trust that He will keep His promise. In obedience to His Word, we become active as we go out to apply for jobs. We could say that the visible side of our faith is our unshakable, active walk toward a goal, which is the implementation of God's will.

This brings us to the other three ingredients in the faith topic: prayer, pain and perseverance. Prayer, in itself, could be seen as an act of faith. Since our God is invisible, we can only trust and accept by faith that, in accordance to His Word, He hears our prayers, and also answers our requests. In the following chapter we will talk more about the important subject of prayer.

Pain is an inevitable part of our faith journey. The beautiful flower garden of faith is watered with sorrow and perseverance. The problems we face in our lives cause us to reflect deep within ourselves, which often brings forth fruit for eternity. It is the refining fire of our trials and tribulations that builds the required quality in us to do God's work effectively:

> "My brethren, count it all joy when ye fall into divers temptations; Knowing this, that the trying of your faith worketh patience. But let patience have her perfect work, that ye may be perfect and entire, wanting nothing" (Js.1:2-4).

Pain teaches us to live by faith rather than by our circumstances. We could say that "adversity produces maturity", and that faith is the climbing-rope with which we can get past those obstacles in our lives.

One of the greatest examples of faith found in the Bible is Joseph, who persevered under incredible challenges, and in the end became all that God had promised him. It was his unbreakable faith, the trusting that God would keep His promise, that sustained him. Someone once suggested that "present problems are often the preparation for future positions", as is very evident in Joseph's life. The birthing of the implementation of God's sovereign will is generally preceded by a time of intensive labour. The fact that we might not be quite ready at times to handle God's promise according to His will, often brings the time-factor into the picture. When the Lord asked Moses to lead the Israelites out of Egypt, they didn't just quickly pack up their belongings and leave. It took some time of heavy labouring before God's purpose was finally accomplished. And like many of us, the Israelites became very discouraged when God's promise was not instantly fulfilled. "Did God really say that He wants to free us? Did He really speak to Moses? What if Moses didn't understand correctly? What if we are being deceived...?"

The faith journey is definitely not an easy one, as the Lord is continually challenging and purifying us. So we learn that it is the combination of suffering and perseverance that will produce a lasting change of great quality in a person. Just like carbon under pressure changes over time and becomes a most valuable diamond, reflecting the beautiful colours of the sunlight; in the same way, a Spirit-filled believer, enriched and changed through life's pressures, reflects the beautiful colours of the light and character of the Son of God.

Rather than to constantly stare at our goals and dreams, we must learn to value and embrace the road that it takes to get there. The refining process, which is the path, is what really counts. It is the trying and testing of our faith that purifies our motives, and it is our hardship that solidifies our faith.

"People of unshakable vision and indefatigable perseverance are those who have been with the Lord long enough, consistently enough, and deeply enough to know that He delights to help us accomplish the impossible dreams He gives us."

(Author unknown)

The visible side of our faith is
our unshakable, active walk
toward a goal.

Chapter 12

Prayer – Connecting With God

LIFE IS ABOUT RELATIONSHIPS. First and fore-most, it is about a person's relationship with the Creator, and then with people. A key factor in any relationship is the ability to meaningfully communicate. Proper, valuable communication has become a rare commodity in our western culture. For many, to communicate at all appears to be a great challenge when we look at the numbers of a fairly recent statistic. Here we read that married couples, after three years of marriage, talk for an average of only a few min-utes during the course of a day. Then there is the survey telling us how much time people spend in front of their TV or computer...

The lack of communication, not only in mar-riages, leads to all kinds of problems. Soon peo-ple's opinions are based on what they guess and assume rather than on verified facts. And for those who still do communicate, the wide-spread inability to listen attentively hinders quality communication. It also seems, many could use some training in how to talk *with* peo-ple, rather than about them. (Then there are those who only want to talk when they have a problem or when they need something.)

We could say that the way we talk with others reflects how we relate. In other words: shallow communication equals shallow relationship; no communication equals no relationship.

And what about our communication skills in our most important relationship? When, how, and why are we talking with Jesus–if we are talking? How are we doing with the development of our "spiritual ears"? Are we able to listen attentively? Maybe we don't really want to listen since His answers are not always so pleasing to us. Why does He answer the way He does anyway? Some of us have given up prayer altogether because God's answers either didn't seem to come at all, or were too hard to swallow. Perhaps we thought since God knows everything, it is not really necessary to squeeze prayer into our busy schedule.

The following Scriptures give us an idea of what the Lord has in mind in regards to prayer:

> "Praying always with all prayer and supplication in the Spirit, and watching thereunto with all perseverance and supplication for all saints" (Eph.6:18).
> "Pray without ceasing" (1Th.5:17).
> "I will therefore that men pray every where, lifting up holy hands, without wrath and doubting" (1Tim.2:8).

We are told to pray at all times, with faith and with passion. In Luke 18:1, Jesus personally commands us to always pray without giving up. It seems that we don't have an option. The Lord wants us to pray! The fact is, we cannot have a meaningful relationship with Jesus Christ without regularly communicating with Him.

But why, if prayer is so important, does God not answer our requests? Let me say that the Lord always answers when we earnestly pray. It's just that He does it in His timing and fashion. We need to continually be reminded that His ways are not ours, and that He is the one in charge:

> "For my thoughts are not your thoughts, neither are your ways my ways, saith the Lord" (Is.55:8).

"Where wast thou when I laid the foundations of the earth" (Job 38:4)?

So when we question why God doesn't answer our prayers, or why His answers seem to seldom reflect our requests; rather than cease communicating, we should consider changing our approach.

Many of us, after we accepted Christ, asked Him in our initial excitement to take our life and do whatever He wants with us. The next thing that followed was a "wish-list" we gave to Him in prayer, with all of our dreams and desires, including the things we needed Jesus to fix for us. Then we waited for Him to fulfill our requests. When He didn't answer the way we expected Him to, we began to wonder if our list got lost in the mail on its way to Heaven, or if the Lord was on holidays when we prayed. But what if He really did answer our prayer–the one where we asked Him to do whatever He wants with our life?

It is important for us to understand that when we get saved, when we ask Jesus to take everything into His hands, we become His "project". He immediately begins to work on us, trying to develop us into the people He wants us to be. This is a very individual and complex process, depending on who we are and what our background is. He is the only one who knows exactly what it takes for us to become that new person. Also, things are generally a little more involved than we think they are. It gets really complicated as God works not just in us and through us; but at the same time, in and through others around us.

Time is a big factor when it comes to our personal development and healing. Prayer and patience are inseparably connected for the enhancement of our faith. I believe that is why God's most-given answer to our problems and requests consists of these three words: "Just trust me!" The Lord is usually not interested in "a quick fix" the way we would like to see it. Our fast-food, drive-through mentality causes us a lot of stress as we ask "Now"!

We are also an incredibly stubborn people when it comes to change and growth. Most of us, in order to become compatible with God's plan, even have to be "broken" so that He can make us new. May we always remember that God is for us, and that whatever He does in our lives is born out of a deep and true love, and full of His infinite wisdom.

God may not answer your prayers the way you hoped He would; but if you truly leave your requests with Him in faith, He will give you peace and strength to accept His sovereign decision in the matter.

I mentioned earlier that the Lord always blesses His goals and not ours. God is the one who sees the big picture, and He has traveled the future. What we really need to ask again is what our prayer requests are based on. Are they a list of selfish wants, or God-inspired desires? Is our intimate, mature relationship with Jesus Christ behind our prayers, or are we still driven by our flesh and our worldly ambitions? The truth is, when we ask for something that is not according to His will, we are asking in vain. When our prayers bounce back at us, it's not because God doesn't care; but it's most often because our requests are not in line with what He wants to do. The Christian life is about Christ and His will, not about us and our wants. Let us also consider that the Lord, by not answering the way we would like, might want to protect us just as a father protects his child. Not only does He know what is best, what our needs are and what the future holds, but He also loves us very much.

The real problem concerning our prayer-life is not so much the way God answers or doesn't answer our prayers, but it is our struggle as we are trying to swim against the current of His plan for our lives. That is why communicating with God in prayer should be a reflection of what He wants to accomplish: "*Thy kingdom come. Thy will be done in earth, as it is in heaven*" (Matt.6:10).

Mature prayer is not just talking to Jesus, or giving Him a Santa-list of things we think we need, (the Lord is not a vending machine where we throw in a quick prayer and out comes the blessing). Mature prayer is rather connecting with Him regarding His plan. And how can we know what He wants to do or what His plan is? Two things are needed: the studying of God's Word and a close relationship with the Lord. The level of our knowledge of His sovereign will correlates directly with the level of intimacy we have reached in our relationship with Jesus Christ through His Holy Spirit. When we give ourselves unconditionally to Him, we will be able to know and also prove His will:

"*I beseech you therefore, brethren, by the mercies of God, that ye present your bodies a living sacrifice...; and be not conformed to this world: but be ye trans-*

formed by the renewing of your mind, that ye may prove what is that good, and acceptable, and perfect, will of God" (Rom.12:1,2).

Sometimes the only way we can learn to really become thirsty for God and His will is when He leads us into the desert for a while. It is our intimacy with Jesus that turns our self-focused ambitions into a God-focused lifestyle. Such a relationship with our Lord will broaden our perspective, enabling us to see through God's eyes the big picture of His plan for our personal lives, our communities, our nation, and even the world. And it is the knowledge of His will, through His Word and the counsel and conviction of His Holy Spirit, that works as a natural adjustment for our prayer requests. Not my will, but Your will be done!

Becoming more and more God-focused, we realize that He wants us to be His workers in the soul harvest, which does not allow us to continue to live in our small world of personal desires and requests. Once we've made the decision to get in on God's bigger plan, our prayer-life will dramatically change. And when our prayers reflect that we truly seek His Kingdom first in everything, He will bless us with an exciting life, full of His purpose, and He will also add a few extra things:

"But seek ye first the kingdom of God, and His righteousness; and all these things shall be added unto you" (Matt.6:33).

As we delight ourselves in the Lord, He promises to give us the desires of our heart, because they are in tune with His will: *"Delight thyself also in the Lord; and He shall give thee the desires of thine heart"* (Ps.37:4).

This brings us to the most critical reason why prayer is so very important; the prayers of God's people are an essential ingredient in the accomplishment of His will here on earth. Positive change only happens when Christians earnestly pray. As mentioned before, from the beginning of mankind, God has chosen to work with and through people in order to fulfill His sovereign plan. He used Joseph to save his family from starvation. He used Moses to lead the Israelites out of captivity. He even used some pretty ordinary folks (people who went fishing for a living or who worked in the government's revenue department for example), to start the first church, to spread the Gospel and to record God's Word.

The Lord is a relational God, and He is a God of love. In fact, He *is* love! And He is also a God of high-quality standards, not interested in a shallow or legalistic relationship with us, based on rules and regulations. Therefore, the quality of our relationship with Him is the free choice He gives us, to love Him and to work with Him, *"for we are labourers together with God"* (1Cor.3:9).

It seems most of us appreciate the love part of our relationship with Jesus, but we are lacking understanding when it comes to our working relationship. Maybe it's a little bit like this: Picture a huge, mysterious insurance company owned by J. Christ, called "Real Life Insurance Un-Ltd." After we hear about the company's absolutely free, no strings attached insurance deal, we go to pick up our free package. We are told to carefully read the life manual and apply it for our benefit, and that whenever we are ready, the owner would like to meet with us regarding His also free and exciting partnership offer. After we've expressed our gratitude for the free real life insurance, we go home, put the life manual on the top shelf, and go back to our regular routine of making a living. Soon we forget about the invitation to become an active member of J. Christ's Company. Unfortunately, since our busy schedule didn't allow us to carefully study the life manual, we never learned about the exciting reward system established for those who become partners in the real life insurance business. For everything we do for the company, there will be a savings deposit waiting for us in "the Bank of Heavenly Rewards".

The issue of investing into God's Kingdom has been widely ignored and misunderstood in the Christian community. Yet, when we think of the persecution of Christians during the early church days, it was most likely their awareness of heavenly rewards that kept them going in spite of their circumstances:

> "Rejoice, and be exceeding glad: for great is your reward in heaven"(Matt.5:12).
> "For the Son of man shall come in the glory of His Father with His angels; and then He shall reward every man according to his works" (Matt.16:27).
> "Now He that planteth and He that watereth are one: and every man shall receive his own reward according to his own labour. For we are labourers together with God"(1Cor.3:8,9).
> "Knowing that of the Lord ye shall receive the reward of the inheritance: for ye serve the Lord Christ"(Col.3:24).
> "And, behold, I come quickly; and my reward is with

me, to give every man according as his work shall be"(Rev.22:12).

It definitely pays to save up some treasures in Heaven, especially since we will be spending eternity there. I am sure there will be a disappointing moment for those who had a lot of earthly possessions and didn't put enough effort into some heavenly deposits.

Let me state very clearly that our earned rewards in Heaven are in no way connected with our salvation. Whether or not we work in His business does not have any affect on our redemption. Our salvation is solely based on what Jesus has done for each one of us on the cross, and our free ticket to Heaven is guaranteed and signed with His blood:

> *"For by grace are ye saved through faith; and that not of yourselves: it is the gift of God: Not of works, lest any man should boast" (Eph.2:8,9).*
> *"For I am persuaded, that neither death, nor life, nor angels, nor principalities, nor powers, nor things present, nor things to come, nor height, nor depth, nor any other creature, shall be able to separate us from the love of God, which is in Christ Jesus our Lord" (Rom.8:38,39).*

We could look at God's offer to become an active partner in His work as a bonus on top of the free gift of real life. He loves us so much that He wants to share with us in His ventures. There are no prerequisites as far as our abilities, our formal education, or our family background. Anyone is welcome to join the business. And because the Lord is not only a loving, but also a just God, He is even going to pay us for our labour:

"For God is not unrighteous to forget your work and labour of love, which ye have showed toward His Name, in that ye have ministered to the saints, and do minister" (Heb.6:10).

What an exciting and incredible privilege it is to be invited to play a vital part in the implementation of God's plan for mankind. There is no greater joy and honour than to share in His business.

But the Lord, through His invitation to work together with us, has limited Himself. He depends very much on our cooperation and our level of commitment to Him. Let me try to give a practical illustration of how our working relationship with Him functions on a personal level. God may have given someone an outstanding musical talent. Now this person's part in the deal is to buy an instrument and practice daily, possibly pursuing the calling to become a worship leader.

The Lord has created all of us with a certain measure of different talents and special abilities. The fact that He has made us should eliminate any form of pride and competition:

"Having then gifts differing according to the grace that is given to us..."(Rom.12:6).
"And unto one He gave five talents, to another two, and to another one; to every man according to his several ability..." (Matt.25:15).

When it comes to our involvement in God's work, we should never assume that we have to be super-professional for the Lord to use us. He is not looking for perfection or professionalism; all He is interested in is our availability, our willingness to be used by Him in any capacity. It is His Holy Spirit who will equip us with what it takes to pursue our individual calling and to do the work He has prepared for each one of us.

Now let us take a closer look at how all of this relates to our prayer life and the accomplishment of God's sovereign plan on earth. Prayer, although one of the jobs in His business that every Christian is capable of doing, is probably the most neglected and underestimated one, at least in our part of the world. Anything that happens or doesn't happen on this earth is directly linked to the prayers of God's people. When we pray for God's will to be done, when His concern becomes our concern, we automatically show our allegiance to Him. He then disburses His power to us so that we can do His work effectively:

> "But ye shall receive power, after that the Holy Ghost is come upon you: and ye shall be witnesses unto me both in Jerusalem, and in all Judaea, and in Samaria, and unto the uttermost part of the earth" (Acts 1:8).

And since God is almighty and all-knowing, He knew from the beginning of time what it would take to accomplish His will. I believe the Lord arranged in advance everything that is needed to fulfill His purpose here on earth. Whether it is concerning our personal lives, our communities, or our countries, it's already all in the storehouse of Heaven. Now it is up to us to do our part in the working relationship, which is to cause the delivery of those things prepared to achieve His goals and purpose. When we pray for something that we know is also His will, He promises to give it to us:

> "And this is the confidence that we have in Him, that,
> if we ask anything according to His will, He heareth
> us: And if we know that He hear us, whatsoever we
> ask, we know that we have the petitions that we
> desired of Him" (1Jn.5:14,15).

The prophet Daniel gives us a good example of how to pray for something that is already in the storehouse. As Daniel was reading how the Lord had spoken to the prophet Jeremiah, concerning the captivity of Daniel and his people, he realized that their time under Babylonian authority was coming to an end. God had promised to restore and bring them back after seventy years. When Daniel began to pray for the release of his people, he prayed for something that was already promised by God (see Jer. 25,29; Dan.9).

From Daniel's example we learn that the Lord doesn't just deliver His promises while we are sitting and waiting. Again, God wants to work with us. Collaboration is the key in the accomplishment of His will. The Lord did His part. Daniel's part was to find out what God's plan was, and then get in on it by prayer and supplication, and with great faith.

The storehouse principle is even more evidently seen in our salvation. When Jesus took His last breath on the cross of Calvary, more than two thousand years ago, He made the most significant deposit in the storehouse that would impact mankind forever: His very own blood. With the words "It is finished", He basically stated that salvation was now in the storehouse of Heaven, waiting and ready to be delivered to anyone who would ask for it.

We could say that effective prayer is the energy which sets in motion the delivery of the implementation of God's sovereign plan. And it is the Lord who has predetermined how much energy it takes. In other words, different things require different amounts of prayer. On one occasion, also recorded in the book of Daniel 10:12 and 13, the prophet prayed for twenty-one days before the answer finally arrived. Jesus, through His Holy Spirit, will put on our hearts how, and how much to pray in a specific situation. The following Scriptures are wonderful guidelines for an effective prayer life:

"The effectual fervent prayer of a righteous man availeth much" (Js.5:16).

"Ye ask, and receive not, because ye ask amiss, that ye may consume it upon your lusts" (Js.4:3).

"But let him ask in faith, nothing wavering. For he that wavereth is like a wave of the sea driven with the wind and tossed"(Js.1:6,7).

"Therefore I say unto you, what things soever ye desire, when ye pray, believe that ye receive them, and ye shall have them" (Mk.11:24).

"But when ye pray, use not vain repetitions, as the heathen do: for they think that they shall be heard for their much speaking. Be not ye therefore like unto them: for your Father knoweth what things ye have need of, before ye ask Him" (Matt.6:7,8).

"Evening, and morning, and at noon, will I pray, and cry aloud: and He shall hear my voice" (Ps.55:17).

"Praying always with all prayer and supplication in the Spirit, and watching thereunto with all perseverance and supplication for all saints" (Eph.6:18).

"But ye, beloved, building up yourselves on your most holy faith, praying in the Holy Ghost. Keep yourselves in the love of God, looking for the mercy of our Lord Jesus Christ unto eternal life" (Jd. 1:20,21).

Our Lord Jesus has great and exciting things in store for those who choose to play on His team. He is not limited by our poor imagination. His desire is to give us a meaningful life, filled with His purpose and blessed with heavenly rewards. May we all become partners in God's business as we get in on His wonderful plan for our personal lives, our communities, our nation, and even the world.

When we come to understand that our human life is but a breath in the light of eternity; when life here on earth becomes nothing more than camping for a while, and the storms and the rain, even the sunshine can't draw our hearts away from the place at His feet; it is then that our intimacy with Jesus will shape our prayers to become a reflection of our longing for His Kingdom to come and for His will to be done on earth as it is in Heaven.

Positive change only happens when Christians earnestly pray.

Chapter 13

The Road to Revival

IMAGINE THIS SCENARIO, it is Saturday evening, time to get ready for church. It's been a while since our church leaders decided to start a Saturday church service. A group of radical, no-compromise people in our church have been praying and fasting for quite some time, when finally the pastor decides to start an extra service on Saturdays. The congregation is large enough, and a Saturday service allows those to come who usually have to work on Sundays. However, the main emphasis would still be the regular Sunday morning service. Unfortunately, the limited time and the structured program doesn't really allow the Holy Spirit to move freely. Also, those with a prophetic gift strongly sense that the Lord is about to do something new and exciting, and that it is time to press in on God through corporate worship and prayer like never before.

The first few Saturdays, although quite different from the regular Sunday routine, were very exciting, but nothing in comparison to what is taking place now...

It all began with an older fellow who walked up to the microphone one Saturday night. All he said was, "I'm sorry, Jesus", and then he went down on his knees, sobbing almost uncontrollably. What really made this an outstanding event was that about fifty people joined him that night. They were crying and repenting as they fell to their knees before the Lord.

The following Saturdays saw the whole congregation on their faces crying out to God for His mercy, and for His glory to be revealed. Then it happened... Some felt a warm breeze touch their faces or saw a bright light engulfing the room. Others heard a sound or sensed a sweet aroma surrounding them...

Ever since God's Holy Spirit came in His power, we have been witnessing the most incredible manifestations. People are receiving physical and emotional healing as they fall down onto the floor, unable to stand in His powerful presence. Many have rededicated their lives to the Lord after they spent hours repenting and pouring out their hearts to Jesus. But what is most exciting about all of this is that people are lining up in front of the church to get into one of our (now five) services. Hundreds have accepted Jesus as their Saviour and many more are added during every service. God is drawing people like a magnet into the church. There have even been reports from those who didn't know the Lord, who, as they were driving by, felt an unexplainable urge to stop and come in. After they received Jesus, they knew that it was His Holy Spirit leading them.

Revival! The spiritual awakening of the church through the reviving of the people in their passion for Jesus. When God's Holy Spirit comes in His power, pouring down from Heaven as living water, He brings new life, and His overwhelming presence is revealed through the signs and miracles that only He can do:

"And he showed me a pure river of water of life, clear as crystal, proceeding out of the throne of God and of the Lamb. In the midst of the street of it, and on either

side of the river, was there the tree of life, which bare
twelve manner of fruits, and yielded her fruit every
month: and the leaves of the tree were for the healing
of the nations" (Rev.22:1,2).
"Jesus answered and said unto her, If thou knewest the
gift of God, and who it is that saith to thee, Give me to
drink; thou wouldest have asked of Him, and He would
have given thee living water" (Jn.4:10).

It is not the sophisticated sermon of a well-trained preacher, or the professional sound and musicianship of a worship band, nor is it the waving of flags or the dancing of dancers that will bring victory to the church. Just like Moses was forever changed after he went up on the mountain to meet with God, so also His people today must have a personal encounter with Him. Only when we are enveloped in God's Shekinah Glory presence will we be transformed, healed, empowered and authorized to become true representatives of Jesus Christ.

In the introduction of this chapter I tried to paint a picture of what an "outbreak" of revival could possibly look like. We can easily see why a church revival is in God's greatest interest, when we understand that it is always accompanied by a large soul harvest. It is believed that the great American revival in 1859, for example, generated as many as half a million Christians in one year. The saving of souls is the very reason why Christ gave His life on the cross of Calvary; and when the Christian church radiates the Shekinah Glory of God, people are drawn by His supernatural presence.

Since the 18th century, there have been many reports of revivals all around the world. However, in the past decade we have witnessed a noticeable increase of God's powerful move in the church. This doesn't come as a surprise for those who strongly believe that we live in the last days of the end time. Many even expect that, in the near future, we will see the greatest outpouring of His Holy Spirit in the history of the church, igniting a soul harvest of unspeakable dimensions:

> "And it shall come to pass in the last days, saith God, I will pour out of my Spirit upon all flesh: and your sons and your daughters shall prophesy, and your young men shall see visions, and your old men shall dream dreams" (Acts 2:17).

Seeing that God's main concern for mankind is most definitely salvation, we might want to ask why we don't experience more revivals, and what the role of the church is in the overall revival picture? In order to understand the dynamics in this matter, we have to go back to some of the essentials regarding our relationship with the Lord.

In the previous chapter we talked about how God wants to work with us in the accomplishment of His purpose:

> "For we are labourers together with God" (1Cor.3:9).
> "For we are His workmanship, created in Christ Jesus unto good works, which God hath before ordained that we should walk in them" (Eph.2:10).

We also saw that, since the Lord is all-knowing, He knew from the beginning of time what it would take to fulfill His will. It can therefore be assumed that God's part in the revival business has already been completed; it's already in the storehouse of Heaven. It is now up to us to do our part, which is to get in on His harvest plan. The question is, what must we as Christians do so that revival will be delivered from the store-house? The answer to this question, although challenging, will not be surprising to most of us: The road to revival is paved with many, many prayers; prayers of true repentance! These prayers, in order to be effective, must have their roots in a holy fear of God. Our love for Jesus can only be true if it co-exists with a deep sense of respect for our Saviour and His values:

> "Only fear the Lord, and serve Him in truth with all your heart: for consider how great things He hath done for you" (1Sam.12:24).
> "For as the heaven is high above the earth, so great is His mercy toward them that fear Him" (Ps.103:11).
> "He will fulfil the desire of them that fear Him" (Ps.145:19).
> "The Lord taketh pleasure in them that fear Him" (Ps.147:11).
> "Happy is the man that feareth always" (Prov.28:14).

The Lord isn't just a compassionate, forgiving and loving father-friend. As the God of the whole universe, He is also a great King and Ruler, who is almighty in His power! Most of us like to embrace only the attributes of love and compassion we see in God, not realizing that it is His other characteristic that will free us from the devil: "The lion hath roared, who will not fear? The Lord God hath spoken, who can but prophesy?" (Amos 3:8)

To fear the Lord, which is nothing other than the result of a mature understanding of His love and His sovereignty, is something that seems to have been swallowed up in our modern day church by a deceptive concept of God's grace. Misinterpreting His love and mercy, many believers have concluded that some of the Lord's principles and commands are mere suggestions and therefore optional, (surveys, showing that the divorce rate among Christian couples is higher than with non-believers, confirms this). We need to realize that just because Jesus brought salvation to us doesn't mean that God's Holy standards and values have changed. He still hates sin, and a lukewarm Christian walk makes Him feel as sick today as it did during the time of the Laodicean Church.

Culminating in a widespread *laissez faire* attitude regarding our Christian conduct, our lack of such a holy fear has caused us to drop our guard, subjecting ourselves to all kinds of evil attacks, for example, the spirit of compromise and adultery with the world:

> "Ye adulterers and adulteresses, know ye not that the friendship of the world is enmity with God? Whosoever therefore will be a friend of the world is the enemy of God" (Js.4:4; see also 1Jn.2:15-17).

We must open our eyes to the deception we have fallen into. It is impossible for us to have a close, intimate relationship with Jesus, as long as we keep competing on the world's stage, trying to get the most out of this life. Our worldly desires and ambitions easily become our motivation, our main focus in life, thus making us an enemy of God. Without the help, council, and protection of His Holy Spirit, we are like sheep without a shepherd, waiting to be devoured. We should never forget that satan is real, and that we are in a spiritual battle. To wear an armour that is not fully intact, or not even there at all, makes us more than vulnerable to be mislead by the devil.

One of the biggest problems in the church today is that Christians are too comfortable, not at all encouraged to develop a healthy fear of God. Most of us think that going to church should in no way be a challenging or a stretching experience. We like to feel comfortable in a user-friendly environment, with a nice atmosphere. Is this what church is about? We won't find the non-challenging church style idea advertised in God's Word; and Jesus Himself, although He was love personified, never intended to make anyone feel comfortable:

"I am come to send fire on the earth. Suppose ye that I am come to give peace on earth? I tell you, nay; but rather division" (Lk.12:49,51).

The Gospel of Jesus Christ is not just about love, forgiveness and freedom, but it is also the serious truth that makes the difference between life and death. It is the Holy Spirit-anointed message of God's powerful living Word that will generate quality believers, as it cuts deep, like a double-edged sword, into the heart of man:

"For the Word of God is quick, and powerful, and sharper than any two-edged sword, piercing even to the dividing asunder of soul and spirit, and of the joints and marrow, and is a discerner of the thoughts and intents of the heart" (Heb.4:12).

This is why someone who has been genuinely saved cannot keep on sinning without major conviction from the Holy Spirit weighing heavily on his heart. Only when we are challenged and convicted by His Spirit and through His Word, will we be motivated to become sincere in our Christian walk. (If we would have just a glimpse of what He has saved us from, we would find it quite easy to develop a real passion for Jesus!)

I firmly believe the Lord is withholding His abundant blessings from the church as long as we keep adding a little bit of Jesus to our busy lifestyles; as long as we are focusing too much on people rather than on God and His Word; and as long as there is hidden, un-confessed sin among us. By compromising our call to be His, and His alone, we have caused ourselves to miss out on the most incredible and fulfilling God-life that He wants to give each one of us:

> "And Elijah came unto all the people, and said, How long halt ye between two opinions? If the Lord be God, follow Him: but if Baal, then follow him" (1K.18:21).
> "...choose you this day whom ye will serve" (Josh.24:15).

The earnest decision to make Jesus Christ the centre of our lives, and to show our desperate need for His Spiritual Counsellor is inevitable, if we want to see a life-changing move of God in our personal lives, and also in the church in general. To see some dramatic changes requires some dramatic actions! When we wholeheartedly surrender all to Jesus, His Holy Spirit will ignite in us the fire of true passion for our Saviour; a fire that will purify our motives, and that will burn down the walls of deception and religion.

The key is to become and to stay close with our Lord through His Spirit. God's promise is to draw near to us when we draw near to Him:

> "Submit yourselves therefore to God. Resist the devil, and he will flee from you. Draw nigh to God, and He will draw nigh to you" (Js.4:7,8).

Our intimacy with the Lord is absolutely essential when it comes to knowing His will. The more we love Jesus, the closer and deeper our walk becomes with Him; the clearer we will hear from Him, and the more we will hear from Him.

Nevertheless, becoming intimate with Christ also means getting closer to the standard of perfect righteousness, which puts everything, our lives and our relationship with God, in perspective. In His holy presence, our sinfulness is magnified, and we see ourselves as we truly are, sinners saved by grace. This will ultimately lead to an attitude of repentance, regardless of the fact that all of our sins have been forgiven through His blood sacrifice. (Our habit of doing wrong was obviously not automatically eliminated when Jesus had "finished" His salvation plan on the cross.)

Unfortunately, the issues of repentance and humble confession, as well as the fear of the Lord, have been either brushed aside or seen as unsophisticated in today's church. We usually prefer to avoid these subjects. Many Christians seem to think that, when we decide to humble ourselves and repent, it implies we are going to enter the land of heavy hearts and sad faces. Taking the step of confession may not be easy, but it is most certainly very rewarding. To repent simply means to deliberately change a course from wrong to right, which can only be a positive, freeing experience. When we honestly love the Lord, daily confession will become a standard ingredient in our worship lifestyle because it will grieve us every time we disappoint the One who gave His life for us. This attitude will not only allow us to develop humble and grateful hearts, but we will also come to enjoy the freedom His forgiveness brings:

> "He that covereth his sins shall not prosper: but whoso confesseth and forsaketh them shall have mercy" (Prov.28:13).

Our active confession will lead to personal healing, but it will also bring healing to the church. In the book of Jeremiah 15:19, the Lord promises to restore those who repent. It is the attitude of repentance that reflects our maturity and our love for Jesus, as it shows that we understand who we really are, and what He has saved us from. Such a humble disposition is obviously pleasing to God, and it will cause the delivery, not only of His freedom from our guilt and shame, but also of the many good things God has in store for those who walk humbly:

> "Humble yourselves in the sight of the Lord, and He shall lift you up" (Js.4:10).
> "Whosoever therefore shall humble himself as this little child, the same is greatest in the kingdom of heaven; ...and he that shall humble himself shall be exalted" (Mat.18:4;23:12).

King David is a prime example of what it means to live with the humble attitude of confession. He was a sinner just like everyone else; but he was also quick to repent and the Lord called him "...a man after mine own heart..." (Acts13:22). This shows that humility, commonly misunderstood, is not at all a sign of weakness. As most of us know, David was far from being a weakling; he spent a good part of his life with a sword in his hand, fighting.

Now let us look at the three different kinds of repentance necessary in order to attain personal freedom and healing, as well as the healing and the empowerment of the church.

The first level of repentance on our list is personal repentance, the most basic and common one, applied when we get saved and when we commit a personal sin. The next one is a little more sophisticated as it involves sins not personally committed. The sins of our forefathers or our family, for example. The prophet Nehemiah and his people confessed the sins of their fathers:

"And the seed of Israel separated themselves from all strangers, and stood and confessed their sins, and the iniquities of their fathers" (Neh.9:2).

At this point I would like to draw our attention to a very important principle. Sin doesn't just somehow disappear or go away, and there is also no hiding place for it. The Lord hates sin, and He could never ignore it, or just forget about it. All sin, according to God's Holy and righteous standards, must eventually be brought out of its darkness into the light of His righteousness where it will be sentenced. God's Holiness simply doesn't allow any form of sin in His universe.

This leads us to another principle. Remember our working relationship with Jesus, and also the free choice He gives us? By dying for us, the Lord made the forgiveness of sin available, He did not force it on us! When Jesus went to the cross for the sin of the world, He created a disposal place for sins. The Lord did His part. Now it is up to us to do our part, which is to drop off our bad deeds through confession. The bottom line is, the Almighty God of Heaven does not go out, forcing salvation on people while they are running after their sins, begging them to give themselves to Him; the people must humbly go to God.

Sin is a form of pollution, and there are only two places for sin-disposal; either the cross of Calvary, where it will be erased through the blood of Jesus, or the lake of fire and brimstone, where it will burn forever.

In trying to analyze the issue of sin, it is important for us to recognize that we are dealing with a package containing two very different items. First of all, there is the original sinful act itself; and secondly, there are the negative consequences resulting from it. When we confess a sin and the Lord in His mercy and by His blood erases it, the effects of the sin we committed are not automatically gone as well; we still face the natural consequences for what we did. We could say a bad choice, or a sinful act, lives on in the negative affects that it produces. Fortunately, these natural consequences can be altered through God's supernatural intervention. As we repent from the heart, the Lord extends His grace beyond the forgiveness of the original wrongful act by changing the outcome, sometimes even to the extent where He turns "ashes into beauty" (see Is.61).

Coming back to our forefathers, even though Jesus paid the price for every bad deed committed on this earth, if not appropriately dealt with by taking them to the cross, these sins or strongholds may still be "at work". Every sin and its root, (possibly an evil deceptive spirit), that has not been deliberately chained to the cross through personal confession, is still "at large" until the day it will be ordered to appear before Him. We must understand that time does not erase sin either; again, only Jesus' blood does. Also, the effects of un-confessed sins might be long-term, and therefore passed on to future generations. This could very well explain why so many Christians, although saved and forgiven, still carry some heavy baggage with them. Just as we inherited our sinful nature from Adam and Eve–it is basically in our blood to be sinners– so also the sins of our forefathers, unless inactivated through confession, and then erased by the power of His blood, were somehow passed on. (The Lord graciously takes care only of sins and their effects that have been humbly brought to Him, whether they are personal or inherited.)

Throughout the Bible we read how blessings as well as sinful habits are transferred from one to another generation:

"Keeping mercy for thousands, forgiving iniquity and transgression and sin, and that will by no means clear the guilty; visiting the iniquity of the fathers upon the children, and upon the children's children, unto the third and to the fourth generation"(Ex.34:7).

Looking once more at the prophet Nehemiah, when the fathers of the Israelites did not repent for their sins, Nehemiah and his people had to face the negative consequences of what their fathers did. The same applies for us today. Whether we're thinking about our ancestors or the past leaders of our nations, their wrong choices may cause us a lot of grief many years later.

But why should we ask the Lord to forgive someone else's sins; isn't it hard enough to repent for our own personal sins? By repenting for the iniquities of our ancestors, we pull unconfessed sin out of its dark hiding place into the light of His holiness; and when love rules our hearts as we humbly come before God, we appease Him, and He then will be pleased to alter the negative affects resulting from our fathers' conduct. "...*love covereth all sins*" (Prov.10:12).

It is our love and respect for Jesus and His Holy standards, and also our compassion for those who have sinned against Him, that draws us to our knees: "*Father, forgive them; for they know not what they do*" (Lk.23:34).

The thing that holds us back from going humbly to the cross is pride. We usually try to get away with as little confession as possible. And when it comes to someone else's sin, instead of following Jesus' example, we say that, since we didn't commit that sin, why should we have to repent for it? (I am sure thankful that Jesus obviously didn't think this way, since He took my sins upon Himself!)

God loves us very much, and He wants us to be free to move on in life so that we can be effective for His purpose. By repenting for the sins of our fathers, we are asking that we don't have to live in bondage, forever hampered and stalled by the negative long-term affects of what they did.

The reason it is so important not to think only of our own personal sins when it comes to repentance, is that God looks at the big picture concerning mankind. There are examples in the Bible where the Lord punished a whole nation—adults, children, and even cattle. We must change our thinking and follow the examples of Jesus, Daniel and Nehemiah. Instead of trying to keep score about "who is guilty of what", we all must pick up our crosses, bearing one another's burdens, and also the burdens of our nation. We have been far too self-focused as Christians. Yes, our salvation is a very individual, personal thing between us and Jesus, but we also need to understand that when the Lord is coming back, He is coming for the church in general, which is the bride of Christ:

"Let us be glad and rejoice, and give honour to Him: for the marriage of the Lamb is come, and His wife hath made herself ready" (Rev.19:7).
"So we, being many, are one body in Christ, and every one members one of another" (Rom.12:5).

This leads us to the third kind of repentance, the kind that will get us onto the road of church revival: the corporate, general repentance. It is the powerful corporate prayer of the church in unity that will generate the strength to pull down the strongholds of our enemy, and it is the humble attitude of confession that will bring God's healing to us and to our land:

"If my people, which are called by my name, shall
humble themselves, and pray, and seek my face, and
turn from their wicked ways; then will I hear from
heaven, and will forgive their sin, and will heal their
land" (2Chr.7:14).

Understanding that the main purpose for
revival is to empower the church and to initiate
a large soul harvest, we can see that our focus in
our corporate prayers should be of a more general nature. Our vision in this case is to reach a
whole city, or an area, or maybe even a whole
nation. Therefore, the object of our repentance
should be the sins of all of God's people including the sins committed by our nation. By living
in a certain country we automatically participate in that countries' business, whether we like
it or not. With our Christian tax dollars, abortion
clinics and questionable military operations are
funded. To see a nation healed and set free, the
crimes committed by that nation must be taken
to the cross through humble confession. And
who will humble themselves and repent for
these crimes if not the Christian men and
women of that nation?!

The following Scriptures from the books of
Nehemiah and Daniel are Biblical examples of
such a prayer of confession:

"..hear the prayer of Thy servant, which I pray before
Thee now, day and night, for the children of Israel Thy
servants, and confess the sins of the children of Israel,
which we have sinned against Thee: both I and my
father's house have sinned"(Neh.1:5).
"O Lord, according to all Thy righteousness, I beseech
Thee, let Thine anger and Thy fury be turned away
from Thy city Jerusalem, Thy Holy mountain: because

*for our sins, and for the iniquities of our fathers, O
Lord, hear; O Lord, forgive." "And whiles I was speaking, and praying, and confessing my sin and the sin of
my people Israel, and presenting my supplication
before the Lord my God..."(Dan.9:16-20).*

When we look at these prayers, we find that
they incorporate all three levels of repentance;
the repentance for their own personal sins, the
sins of their forefathers, and the sins of their fellow countrymen.

We could say that our personal revival and the
healing that it brings, is connected with the forgiveness of the sins in our personal lives, including God's gracious dealing with trouble
possibly inherited from our ancestors. Thinking
again of a church revival, we need to look at all
of the members of the church as one corporate
body:

*"There is one body, and one Spirit, even as ye are called
in one hope of your calling; One Lord, one faith, one
baptism, One God and Father of all" (Eph.4:4-6).
"For we being many are one bread, and one body: for
we are all partakers of that one bread" (Cor.10:17).*

As one big church family, we are all related
with each other through the blood of Jesus
Christ. In his letter to the Corinthian church,
Paul compares the church members with a
human body:

*"For the body is not one member, but many. If the foot
shall say, because I am not the hand, I am not of the
body; is it therefore not of the body"(1Cor.12:14,15)?*

When one part of the body is hurting, the whole body is affected by that pain; and when one part commits a sin, the whole body is burdened: *"Bear ye one another's burdens, and so fulfil the law of Christ"* (Gal.6:2). Whether it is abortion, gossip or adultery, any kind of sin found in the body of Christ affects the whole body. This consequently means that we must all take responsibility for the sins committed in our church family, by confessing our faults to one another and to God:

"And if he have committed sins, they shall be forgiven him. Confess your faults one to another, and pray one for another, that ye may be healed"(Js.5:15,16).

Our Lord is pleased when Christians uphold each other instead of pointing fingers. The Old Testament prophets, Nehemiah and Daniel, obviously understood this principle. They felt burdened, not only with their own personal sins, but also with the sins of their people.

Let me tell a little story about someone else who believed in the idea of shared responsibility.

The former New York Mayor, Fiorello La Guardia, took on the office of a police judge once in a while. It is said that one very cold winter day, an old man was brought before him. This man was accused of stealing a loaf of bread from a bakery store. Trying to justify his crime, he explained that his family was starving. The judge replied that his hands were tied, and he had to punish him, because the law didn't allow any exceptions. After La Guardia had sentenced the old man to a fine of ten dollars, he reached into his own pocket saying, "Here is the ten dollars to pay your fine, and now I am going to pardon your sentence." Throwing a ten dollar bill into the man's hat, the judge raised his voice declaring: "I hereby sentence each person in this courtroom to a fine of fifty cents for living in a city where a man has to steal bread in order to eat!" After a clerk had collected almost fifty dollars, he was ordered to give the money to the old man.

The judge in this story punished the people for not taking responsibility for the well-being of their city, i.e. their fellow citizens. The more independent, the more self-focused people become. They are unable to see someone else's needs, and their own need for a Creator-God. We have failed God, not so much because we don't love Him, but because we don't completely depend on Him. It is our self-sufficiency that leads to a prideful attitude, while hardening our hearts. When we look at the church as a community of believers, we easily understand that our independence also hinders us from recognizing our responsibility for the well-being of our church community.

The Lord doesn't want us to live independently, since one day we will all be together in His Heaven anyway. The fact that we are one body, united in Christ, should set us apart from this world; however, it appears that the importance of unity in the church has been greatly underestimated. The Christian life is not a one-man show! Jesus, Himself, gave us a good example of this truth when He called the twelve disciples to be His "co-workers" in the Gospel business. Why can't we see that disunity among Christians is the devil's way of weakening the church? The following is the apostle Paul's exhortation:

> "For ye are yet carnal: for whereas there is among you envying, and strife, and divisions, are ye not carnal, and walk as men? For while one saith, I am of Paul; and another, I am of Apollos; are ye not carnal?"(1Cor.3:3,4)

Earlier in Paul's letter to the members of the Church of Corinth, he refers to them as babies who are still too immature to handle the "meat and potatoes" issues of Christianity. Instead of growing up and focusing on Jesus Christ, they focused on people like Paul and Apollos, while bickering and fighting like little children.

We have been so busy fighting against each other as Christians, that we don't have time to concentrate on the one who is our real enemy–satan. As we are side-tracked, the devil is at work on all levels in our society, trying to establish his world of evil, while cutting down Christian freedom and influence. We as God's people are the ones with the answers for the problems of our countries. No politicians or police force will be able to fight against the attacks of the devil on our nations, because their weapons are carnal. Spiritual weapons are needed to fight against a spiritual force; but we need to remember that satan is not a little weakling who could easily be pushed over. The strongholds in our communities are powerful. It takes more than one pastor, or a handful of dedicated, on-fire Christians, to kick the devil and his demons out of our cities. Only when the church stands united will we be strong enough to break the big and heavy chains of evil in our society; and only when God's people, who are called by His Name, humble themselves and repent will He send revival and heal our land.

A good illustration of the church's division, (and possibly the reason why Jesus Christ hasn't returned yet), is a bride who is not ready for her groom. She is busy running around, arguing with herself about what colour shoes she should wear with her dress, and whether roses or carnations are best for the wedding. Instead of looking out for her groom with anticipation and excitement, celebrating His coming, she is occupied with herself—the many little and unimportant details of style and outward appearance.

What we must realize is that the true reason for the weakness of the church is not so much the disunity itself. Our un-loving, prideful and prejudiced attitudes toward other believers are the cancer that weakens the bride of Christ, as it produces disunity. This behaviour, according to God's Word, is nothing less than sin against His command for us to love one another. We cannot expect the Lord's blessings for the church as long as we don't take His Word seriously. As members of one body, we have hurt ourselves by hurting others. It is time that God's people begin to see where the real enemy is, and that our focus must be the one common denominator, our Lord Jesus Christ. Our true and active repentance, and the forgiveness of those who have been hurt, will tear down the walls of disunity, and also open the door to God's many blessings:

"Behold, how good and how pleasant it is for brethren to dwell together in unity!"(Ps.133:1)
"With all lowliness and meekness, with longsuffering,

forbearing one another in love; Endeavouring to keep
the unity of the Spirit in the bond of peace" (Eph.4:2,3).

The Lord, although He is a trinity, is not divided–so why should we be? His compassion and forgiveness goes out to all peoples equally, and again, since there is only one Heaven, we will eventually all be together. The only thing that assures our place in God's Kingdom is Jesus Christ's sacrifice on the cross, not a specific style of music or fashion, or the doctrine of a certain denomination. Try to imagine Christians fighting in Heaven over issues like dress code, or whether it would be appropriate to sing hymns or upbeat choruses to our King. I am sure we all agree that this is not going to happen. Why not let God judge about these outward things? In His Word we can already get an idea of what the Lord's thoughts are on this subject:

"Judge not according to the appearance, but judge
righteous judgment" (Jn.7:24).
"Whose adorning let it not be that outward adorning of
plaiting the hair, and of wearing of gold, or of putting
on of apparel; But let it be the hidden man of the heart,
in that which is not corruptible, even the ornament of a
meek and quiet spirit, which is in the sight of God of
great price" (1Pe.3:3,4).
"For the Lord seeth not as man seeth; for man looketh
on the outward appearance, but the Lord looketh on the
heart" (1Sam.16:7).

The following words of our Lord Jesus should be taken as a strong advice for all of us:

"Judge not, that ye be not judged" (Matt.7:1).
"Blessed are the peacemakers: for they shall be called
the children of God"(Matt.5:9).

We must learn to appreciate and embrace the differences in our denominations as a gift that reflects God's creativity in us, since we were created in His image. The God of the whole Universe is far too big to fit into the little box some of us would like to build for Him. Instead of looking at life and the church on the basis of our own understanding, we need to ask the Lord to elevate us to a level where we can see things from His perspective. Then will we be able to understand that all who are in Jesus Christ are citizens of Heaven, and that our limited time here on earth is just the preparation for the real life yet to come:

> "I am a stranger in the earth"(Ps.119:19).
> "For to me to live is Christ, and to die is gain"
> (Phil.1:21).

To be one family in Christ isn't just reserved for us in God's Kingdom; and when we all become active in taking responsibility for the welfare of our church family, a deep healing and strengthening of the body of Christ will take place. It is our humility and the confession of our sins that makes us different from the world. The closer we become with our Saviour, the more His likeness rubs off on us. His compassion in us will enable us to sympathize with those who are hurting and burdened in the church community. May our heads become silent, and may our hearts grow to be a never-ending fountain of His love, poured out among us, as we lift each other up!

The love of Jesus Christ has healed us, and His forgiveness has brought us freedom. In His love we find the strength to forgive others and to build bridges between all of God's people. With the help of His Holy Spirit, we will be able to stand united as one body, even as we repent for the sins committed among us. Not only will this bring God's favour to the church, but it will also send a strong message to the devil and the world around us.

I would like to make us aware of another reason why the issue of unity among Christians is so very crucial: our sin and our weakness as believers doesn't affect just us, but it also has a tremendous effect on God's reputation. As Christ's representatives, we need to constantly remember that we carry His precious Name. The non-Christian world is watching us closely, and we can be certain that satan is pointing out every little flaw that he can find in the church. Thinking of the un-saved and their salvation, it is pretty tough to convince these people that to become part of God's family is something they desperately need, when there is strife and discord in the body of Christ:

"By this shall all men know that ye are my disciples, if ye have love one to another" (Jn.13:35).

Throughout the Bible we find many examples of a deep concern for God's reputation. The Prophet Elijah asked the Lord to send fire from heaven because he was jealous for God:

"Hear me, O Lord, hear me, that this people may know that Thou art the Lord. And he said, I have been very jealous for the Lord God of hosts" (1K.18:37;19:10).

Young David became very angry when God was mocked by the Philistines: *"...that all the earth may know that there is a God in Israel"* (1Sam.17:46). Going back to the prophet Daniel, we see that one of the motivating factors for his prayer was his love for God, expressed in his concern for the Lord's precious Name:

"O Lord, hear; O Lord, forgive; O Lord, hearken and do; defer not, for Thine own sake, O my God: for Thy city and Thy people are called by Thy name" (Dan.9:19).

Translated into today's vernacular, what Daniel was basically saying is this: "Lord, as Christians we are known as Your people, but because we have sinned against You and Your Holy standards, we have caused ourselves a lot of trouble. The people are watching us closely, and they see that we are struggling with many problems. They are laughing when we talk about our Almighty God, because we are so weak and powerless."

Let's ask ourselves: when was the last time that we got really upset when the Name of our precious Saviour was put down? The fact is, by discarding His holy values, and by making fun of them, His Name is constantly defiled in our society. The gods of money and sensuality, with their promotional magazines and movies, have been tolerated and endorsed far too long in our countries! Satan is mocking the Christian church and the Name by which we all stand, by degrading us to the level of "just another philosophy", or a hobby we pursue on Sundays. Most politicians regard our sovereign God with the same respect as they regard the idols and wooden images of other religions. In the name of so-called religious freedom, Christians have been made equal with those who worship stones and stars. Instead of following the example of Elijah by calling down fire from Heaven, the devil has managed to assure that we keep busy arguing with each other, while he is slowly chipping away at our Christian rights and influence. It is time that Christians stand up united for the One and only true God, for His reputation, and for His honourable Name. We must ask the Holy Spirit to give us a zeal and a passion for our Lord, like we have not yet known. His excellent Name is worth fighting for!

It all begins with a decision every true follower of Christ has to make, the decision to wholeheartedly surrender our lives, all that we are and all that we have, to Jesus. Only when the things of this world won't matter anymore, will our eyes be able to behold the most incredible treasures God has in store for those who give themselves unconditionally to Him. As we begin to press in on the Lord like never before, He will open the storehouse of Heaven, pouring out upon us everything that is necessary to do the work of God effectively.

Jesus is looking for people who want to be sold out to Him, whose desire is to follow Him without compromise; believers who have come to realize that the things the world has to offer are worth nothing compared to what the Lord wants to give them.

God's invitation to make us partners in His exciting business is still valid. He is on our side when we choose to actively play on His team:

"For the eyes of the Lord run to and fro throughout the whole earth, to show Himself strong in the behalf of them whose heart is perfect toward Him" (2Chr.16:9).

And when we decide to get in on God's harvest plan, He will give us the Elijah boldness, the divine authority to confront Kings and demons, and to conquer in His mighty Name:

"...for God hath not given us the spirit of fear; but of power, and of love, and of a sound mind" (2Tim.1:7)
"... the righteous are bold as a lion"(Prov.28:1).

In Jesus Christ we became children of the Most High, and we were given the keys to the Kingdom of God. Now is the time to rise up from our apathy and take our rightful place as His precious bride! But, while we respond to God's wake-up call, He will first of all lead us to a place where we are united in a deep brokenness before our loving Saviour, where humility becomes the key to His strength; a place where we will humbly pray together...

"Father in heaven, we all fall short of Your glory, for we all have sinned against You. And we know that, according to Your Holy standards, every sin weighs the same. Even the sins of our fathers and our Nation are weighing heavy on us. Heavenly Father we are burdened as a family. We have been deceived in many ways, because we have not taken Your Word seriously. Lord, cleanse us from the guilt and shame of our iniquities. Forgive us for compromising Your values, and for not standing up for that which we know is right. Cleanse us from the shame of sitting back when Your Holy Name is mocked. Lord, create in us a clean heart and a right spirit. Forgive us that, by bickering and fighting with each other, we have dishonoured the

Name by which we all stand, Jesus Christ. Forgive us, Lord, for the pride and prejudice in our hearts. Our unloving and uncaring attitudes have turned many people away from Your precious, life giving Gospel. Father, show us how to bear one another's burdens, and help us to walk in humility and with love in our hearts, so that the world can see Your light in us. Lord, our Nation is in the claws of the enemy. As we come humbly before Your throne, we ask that You would free and heal our land. Jesus, pour out Your Spirit upon us. We can do nothing without You, Holy Spirit. We can't even be hungry for You, Lord, without Your help. Let us drink of Your strength, for we are weak in our own strength. Help us to know and to do Your will. For Your Name's sake, send revival to Your church, Lord, so that the world may know that we serve a mighty God. In the Holy Name of our precious Lord and Saviour, Jesus Christ, we pray. Amen!"

...and suddenly, I feel a warm breeze touching my face, while others see a bright light engulfing the room. Yet others hear a sound or sense a sweet aroma surrounding them...

The road to revival is paved
with many, many prayers;
prayers of true repentance!

Chapter 14

The Vision, the End-Time, and the Shepherd's Voice

IN THE EARLY MORNING hours on November 4, 2000, I believe the Lord revealed to me in a vision, what appears to be the reason for the struggle and the ineffectiveness of the church in the Fraser Valley, which is located east of Vancouver, Canada, in the "Bible belt". The question of why the church is so powerless had been on my heart for a number of years. Many times in the past the Lord had visited me in my sleep, urging me to pray. Expecting yet another prayer session, I got up that night, only to find myself trembling at the intensity and the heaviness of what turned out to be an amazing revelation.

This is the vision that came to me:

I saw a gigantic, dark-coloured bird sitting in the valley. Its position was that of a hawk or an eagle after it catches its prey. With huge wings spread out from the east to the west, the bird covered the valley with a dark shadow like a blanket. The dark shadow represents the oppression and the reason for the spiritual blindness of the people in the valley. Meanwhile, the bird was digging its talons deep into its prey, the Christian church. And just like the prey of an eagle, the church tried to wriggle and fidget its way out of the strong grip. This is the warfare and the prayers of the Saints. Once in a while a breath of foul smoke, like a heavy fog, would come from the bird's sharp-edged beak. These

174 Awakening The Sleeping Giant

are the chains and strongholds on people's lives, the deceptions and the attacks, the crimes and the suicides that plague this valley and also the church.

Then I saw something like crystal clear water, as thick and heavy as oil, trickling down from the clouds onto the bird who was shaking it off. This is God's Holy Spirit. But the water was also running off from the wings onto part of the church, anointing and strengthening those believers who thirst and hunger, who are God's faithful warriors. As more and more heavy water came down, the bird let go of its grip for a brief moment, trying hard to shake it off. This is the anointed warfare, the intercession and the repentance of those who have been fighting for the release of the church from bondage. At this point the Lord reminded me of Elijah's prayer, as I envisioned a ball of fire coming down from the heavens, consuming the sacrifices.

When I saw the bird again, suddenly a floodgate opened with thick and heavy water gushing down onto the animal. With a loud, screaming noise, the bird let go of its prey as it lifted off.

This is the revival of the church.

There are many strongholds in our countries and in the body of Christ. No matter in which part of the world we live, satan and his helpers will try anything to undermine God's work, and to sabotage and inactivate the church. The vision that God gave me, concerning the church in the Fraser Valley, only confirms that we are in a spiritual battle, and that the strongholds are powerful.

But the Lord is not going to sit back, allowing

the devil free reign. Shortly after I had received the vision, He drew my attention to the following Scripture verses; a confirmation to me that revival is in the storehouse of Heaven, ready to be poured out:

> "I will open rivers in high places, and fountains in the midst of the valleys: I will make the wilderness a pool of water, and the dry land springs of water"(Is.41:18). "And a fountain shall come forth of the house of the Lord, and shall water the valley of Shittim"(Joel 3:18).

These Scriptures and other exciting Bible prophesies are of tremendous significance, considering that the time in which we live represents "the end-time".

When we look around in the world today, we see many signs indicating that these are the "last days". The devil is working hard to prepare the way for a one-world government with the anti-Christ as its leader. Many world organizations have already been established to combat the more and more global ecological and economical problems, and to assure peace here on earth. The United Nations (UN), equipped with an independent military force, the World Bank with its immense monetary power, and the World Health Organization (WHO), represent only a few names on a long list of global institutions that bear the hope of many to rid the world of all kinds of troubles. The uniting of fifteen European countries (EU), through the European Parliament in Strasbourg, France, with the European Common Market and the newly created European currency, the Euro, could be a preview of the worldwide system. Some Bible teachers see the growing number of earthquakes and famines in the past twenty years, the migration of Jewish people from all over the world to Israel, and the peace talks in the Middle East as the fulfillment of Biblical end-time prophecies:

> *"For yourselves know perfectly that the day of the Lord so cometh as a thief in the night. For when they shall say, Peace and safety; then sudden destruction cometh upon them"* (1Thes.5:1-3).

And then there is the epidemic increase of HIV and AIDS, as well as the rising problem of strange flu viruses and cancer:

> *"...and what shall be the sign of Thy coming, and of the end of the world? And Jesus answered and said unto them, Take heed that no man deceive you. For nation shall rise against nation, and kingdom against kingdom: and there shall be famines, and pestilences, and earthquakes, in divers places"* (Matt.24:3,4,7).

But there are many more signs of the times. Computer chips, implanted under the skin as a means of tracing and identifying lost pets via satellite, for example, (some car manufacturers offer the same technology as anti-theft and navigation systems). The latest news is that at least ten US citizens have received a similar implant which will provide medical information in the case of an emergency. It really doesn't take a whole lot of imagination to see most people equipped with such a device, for convenient ID, health, banking, and crime prevention purposes. "Just place your hand on a scanner..., never mind a certain three-digit number on your personal ID computer chip..."

Whatever satan has planed for the future, in the way of establishing his kingdom here on earth, his ideas and strategies to fix the rapidly growing global problems the world is facing will sound very convincing; a masterpiece of deception.

When the disciples asked Jesus about the "last days", He also told them a parable:

> "Now learn a parable of the fig tree; When his branch is yet tender, and putteth forth leaves, ye know that summer is nigh: So likewise ye, when ye shall see all these things, know that it is near, even at the doors" (Mat. 24:32,33).
> "And He said also to the people, When ye see a cloud rise out of the west, straightway ye say, There cometh a shower; and so it is. And when ye see the south wind blow, ye say, There will be heat; and it cometh to pass. Ye hypocrites, ye can discern the face of the sky and of the earth; but how is it that ye do not discern this time?" (Lk.12:54-56)

Whether it is our dramatically increased mobility, ever since automobiles and commercial aviation changed the face of the earth, or the tremendous escalation and spreading of knowledge through communication and computer technologies ("...even to the time of the end: many shall run to and fro, and knowledge shall be increased" Dan.12:4); Jesus doesn't want us to be ignorant of the signs of the times. He wants us to clearly see what the hour is, and He wants us to be prepared, ready for His coming.

Possibly the strongest evidence for the Lord's soon return is the emerging of false teachers and prophets in a world hungry for spirituality:

> "And many false prophets shall rise, and shall deceive many"; "...even as there shall be false teachers among you" (Mat.24:11; 2Pe.2:1).

The number of different denominations and cults who all profess to worship the only "real" god is growing steadily in North-America; and the voices among church leaders calling believers to openness and tolerance toward other religions are getting louder and louder. Many speakers have used the platform of a church service to promote the idea of an "Alliance of different Faiths" which would integrate all major world religions:

> "Then if any man shall say unto you, Lo, here is Christ, or there; believe it not. For there shall arise false Christs, and false prophets" (Mat.24:23,24).

The Lord's strong warning not to walk blindly into the pit of sweet-sounding deceptions is resounding in a church, surrounded by a society which is tossed around like a wave in an ocean of dramatic events and changes:

> "Beware lest any man spoil you through philosophy and vain deceit, after the tradition of men, after the rudiments of the world, and not after Christ" (Col.2:8).

Jesus cautions us to see with open eyes the signs that will precede His second coming.

In God's Word we read that, while the devil is working overtime, Jesus will not look on silently. In His mercy, He is going to reveal Himself worldwide through the pouring out of His Holy Spirit:

*"And it shall come to pass in the last days, saith God, I
will pour out of my Spirit upon all flesh: and your sons
and your daughters shall prophesy, and your young
men shall see visions, and your old men shall dream
dreams: And on my servants and on my handmaidens
I will pour out in those days of my Spirit; and they
shall prophesy: And I will show wonders in heaven
above, and signs in the earth beneath"* (Acts 2:17-19).

God knows exactly what time it is, and He
has already begun a powerful, Spirit-anointed
work in many countries around the world. In
China alone, every day thousands of people are
receiving Jesus as their Saviour, and in other
nations, Christianity is spreading like a wildfire.
The church in North America, although very
reserved, is also beginning to slowly respond to
God's Holy Spirit. There are many Christians
today who have heard the voice of the Lord, calling them to break free from religion and,
instead, pursue a personal and intimate relationship with Jesus Christ. More and more
believers receive dreams and visions, as they
wholeheartedly seek God's presence, thirsting
for His living water, the Holy Spirit. The one
vision, that is shared by many, is that of a train
or a stage-coach coming to pick up those followers of Christ who are thirsty and desperately
waiting for a new move of God:

*"...Jesus stood and cried, saying, If any man thirst, let
him come unto me, and drink. He that believeth on me,
as the Scripture hath said, out of his belly shall flow
rivers of living water. But this spake He of the Spirit,
which they that believe on Him should receive"*
(Jn.7:37-39).
"For my people have committed two evils; they have

> *forsaken me the fountain of living waters, and hewed*
> *them out cisterns, broken cisterns, that can hold no*
> *water" (Jer.2:13).*

Let me ask you a few personal questions. When was the last time that you felt really close with Jesus and deeply touched by His presence in your life? How are your church services? Are you experiencing His Spirit moving your heart, or are you going to church out of a routine? How is your relationship with the Lord affecting you? Are you growing in Him, and are you seeing positive changes? Or do you rather feel stuck for quite some time? Could it be that religion has dried up your spirit too? Do you feel tired and empty, thirsty for the only kind of drink that will truly satisfy your soul?

> *"O God, Thou art my God; early will I seek Thee: my*
> *soul thirsteth for Thee, my flesh longeth for Thee in a*
> *dry and thirsty land, where no water is" (Ps.63:1).*
> *"As the hart panteth after the water brooks, so panteth*
> *my soul after Thee, O God. My soul thirsteth for God,*
> *for the living God" (Ps.42:1,2).*

As the end is fast approaching, more and more Christians are stepping out of the dryness of a church bound by tradition, religion and man-made ideas. Believers who, stirred by His Spirit, have set out to find the place of refreshing and empowerment that Jesus offers in His Word:

> *"But whosoever drinketh of the water that I shall give*
> *him shall never thirst; but the water that I shall give*
> *him shall be in him a well of water springing up into*
> *everlasting life" (Jn.4:14).*

Tired of a mediocre Christian walk, and desperately thirsty for His Holy Spirit, they have chosen to escape a lifestyle of complacency and compromise. The decision to leave the past behind, and to step out in faith, has allowed them to follow the voice of their Shepherd, Jesus, as He is leading them out of the desert to the river of living water:

> "My sheep hear my voice, and I know them, and they follow me" (Jn.10:27).
> "And he showed me a pure river of water of life, clear as crystal, proceeding out of the throne of God and of the Lamb" (Rev.22:1).
> "Thou visitest the earth, and waterest it: Thou greatly enrichest it with the river of God, which is full of water" (Ps.65:9).

When we realize that God has so much more in store for His people, and when the empty feeling, and the dryness of our soul, finally cause us to cry out to Him for His refreshing water, He will fulfill His promise and do something new and exciting:

> "Remember ye not the former things, neither consider the things of old. Behold, I will do a new thing; now it shall spring forth; shall ye not know it? I will even make a way in the wilderness, and rivers in the desert. ... to give drink to my people, my chosen. This people have I formed for myself; they shall show forth my praise" (Is.43:18-21).

Once we have tasted the water of life, our love for the Lord becomes new and fresh. And with a deep passion in our hearts, we are drawn to praise and to worship Him with great joy and excitement.

Being filled with His living water also equips us to effectively share the good news of the Gospel of Jesus Christ. Notice how it talks about sharing or preaching from the belly instead of the head:

> "He that believeth on me, as the Scripture hath said, out of his belly shall flow rivers of living water" (Jn.7:38).

This is the blessing He has for us, that we become empowered to participate in His work. Deep down inside we know, as we press on, that we were redeemed for something more than just the purpose of being allowed into Heaven. The Lord has promised many wonderful things to us in His Word, if we wholeheartedly desire to love Him without compromise. Fruit will grow when God's Word finds a good soil in us. And when we consider ourselves to be a dry and thirsty land, He will satisfy our deepest longing with His precious water of life:

> "I stretch forth my hands unto Thee: my soul thirsteth after Thee, as a thirsty land" (Ps.143:6).
> "For I will pour water upon him that is thirsty, and floods upon the dry ground: I will pour my spirit upon thy seed, and my blessing upon thine offspring" (Is.44:3).
> "I am Alpha and Omega, the beginning and the end. I will give unto him that is athirst of the fountain of the water of life freely. He that overcometh shall inherit all things; and I will be his God, and he shall be my son" (Rev.21:6,7).
> "They shall be abundantly satisfied with the fatness of Thy house; and Thou shalt make them drink of the river of Thy pleasures. For with Thee is the fountain of life: in Thy light shall we see light" (Ps.36:8,9).

How exciting it is to know that our God is the God of abundance. He doesn't give us yesterday's blessings, and He doesn't leave us stranded in a dry place. His blessings are new and fresh every day, and His storehouse is full of heavenly gifts and surprises. God's creativity is not limited, and His love is endless. He has purchased us with His own blood, and His desire is to give us a meaningful life, overflowing with joy, and filled with His infinite purpose.

Have you, too, heard the voice of the Shepherd calling you to follow Him to His place of refreshing? Are you ready for a change, a fresh start? Do you want to find freedom and joy in your life? Is His Spirit drawing you out of the stuffy closet of religion?

These truly are the last days. God is challenging all of us, just as Elijah challenged his people, to get real with Him, to make up our minds, and to follow Him without compromise. His call is going out to the nations today, as He is gathering and equipping His people to become effective and empowered true representatives of Jesus Christ.

So do not hesitate any longer, follow His voice! God's promises are true, and His love never fails!

"Ho, every one that thirsteth, come ye to the waters, and he that hath no money; come ye, buy, and eat; yea, come, buy wine and milk without money and without price" (Is.55:1).
"Oh that men would praise the Lord for His goodness, and for His wonderful works to the children of men!" (Ps.107:8)

See you in "The River" for His refreshing and equipping, and then in "The Field" for His harvest.

While we are joyfully awaiting Jesus' soon return, let us overcome the spirit of unbelief; and let us live in the deep knowing that Heaven is really home.

Epilogue

A Prophetic Word; the Call to an Act of Worship

LET ME CLOSE WITH a final Word to encourage all of you who are seeking a new level in their walk with Jesus. When the Israelites came to the Red Sea, the Lord placed a pillar of fire between them and the armies of Pharaoh. The fire was there to protect God's people and it also hindered them from going back. (Let us remember that change, or a new beginning, isn't easy for most people-especially when there are a few obstacles and barriers ahead.) Some of the Jews would have rather gone back into slavery than walking by faith to a distant promised land.

In order to be able to conquer the individual promise God has in store for each one of us, we must first take that step of faith and cross over–leaving our past, our worldly ambitions and desires behind. And for those who have made it to the other side but feel stuck in some kind of a desert; let me encourage you by saying that the time of testing and teaching is only there to prepare you for what's ahead. *"Behold, I will do a new thing; now it shall spring forth; shall ye not know it? I will even make a way in the wilderness, and rivers in the desert"* (Is.3:19).

I believe that Jesus has kept the best Wine for last, and that we must first become that new Wineskin, shaped and tested in the desert, before we will be able to hold the new and fresh anointing which He has promised for the last days. "When the ruler of the feast had tasted the water that was made wine, and knew not whence it was: (but the servants which drew the water knew;) the governor of the feast called the bridegroom, And saith unto him, Every man at the beginning doth set forth good wine; and when men have well drunk, then that which is worse: but thou hast kept the good wine until now" (Jn.2: 9;10). "And no man putteth new wine into old bottles; else the new wine will burst the bottles, and be spilled, and the bottles shall perish. But new wine must be put into new bottles" (Lk. 5:37;38).

These are challenging days as the Lord is beginning to shake the organized church.

So ask yourself, has all of this busy-ness with church activities and programs left you empty and thirsty...? Are you tired of the old routine...? Are you longing for "the NEW"...? Would you like a challenge...? Are you willing to "jump"...? Are you ready for the "first harvest"...? After I had asked the Lord to show me what it will take in the future for believers to effectively do His work, this is what He spoke to me:

"Many have walked on the leading edge and I chose to do some of My work; but this is a new season, a final call before the great day of the trumpet. There will be no more leading edge for I am going to cause you to jump off the edge. Yes, by faith, uncompromising faith, you must trust Me and jump! And as you leave the old ways behind, opening and renewing your mind, you will know that I am doing a new, a final thing. But before you jump you must take off your shoes, for behold, after I will catch you, I am going to set your feet on a truly solid ground;

and I will give you new shoes that you must walk in. Shoes that will lead and empower you for good works. You will walk in the anointing and in the light of My righteousness. You will walk and not faint. You will walk with boldness and authority. You will surely trample on demons and serpents. You will walk on a strait and narrow path; the path that I, the Lord your God, have prepared for you. These are the days of the first harvest, My harvest. For I, Myself, am bringing into My house a people, selected and equipped for war. They will walk and talk in the Spirit, and with great power. They will be My road-crew, making a way in the desert; a strait road to Jerusalem. They will prepare the coming of the Lord, and they will bring in the great second harvest of many souls."

"Awake thou that sleepest, and arise from the dead, and Christ shall give thee light" (Eph. 5:14).

CPSIA information can be obtained
at www.ICGtesting.com
Printed in the USA
LVOW08s1608181116
513605LV00001B/1/P